THE EDUCATIONAL IDEAS

OF

PESTALOZZI

THE
EDUCATIONAL IDEAS
OF
PESTALOZZI

BY

J. A. GREEN, B.A. LOND.
PROFESSOR OF EDUCATION IN THE UNIVERSITY OF SHEFFIELD

Third Impression

GREENWOOD PRESS, PUBLISHERS
NEW YORK

The Library of Congress cataloged this book as follows:

Green, John Alfred, 1867–
    The educational ideas of Pestalozzi, by J. A. Green.   New
York, Greenwood Press ₍1969₎

     xi, 222 p.   23 cm.

     Reprint of the 1914 ed.
     Includes bibliographical references.

     1. Pestalozzi, Johann Heinrich, 1746–1827.   ɪ. Title.

LB628.G7 1969	370.1′0924	78–90147
SBN 8371–2398–4		MARC
Library of Congress	70 ₍12₎	

Originally published in 1914 by W. B. Clive

Reprinted in 1969 by Greenwood Press, Inc., 51 Riverside Avenue,
Westport, Conn. 06880

Library of Congress catalog card number 78-90147
ISBN 0-8371-2398-4

Printed in the United States of America

10 9 8 7 6 5 4 3 2

PREFACE.

In this attempt to expound the fundamental doctrines of Pestalozzi, I have been chiefly indebted to two admirable articles by Wegel in the XXIII and XXIV *Jahrbücher des Vereins für wissenschaftliche Pädagogik*, entitled "Pestalozzi und Herbart." In the vast extent of German Pestalozzian literature, these articles are generally acknowledged to be the most satisfactory critical account of Pestalozzi's doctrines. I have, however, also found the articles relating to the subject in Rein's *Encyclopädisches Handbuch der Pädagogik* very helpful.

In addition, I have made considerable use of Schmid's *Geschichte der Erziehung*, Vol. IV., Part 2; Schmidt's *Geschichte der Pädagogik*, Vol. IV., by Dr. Richard Lange; Hunziker's *Geschichte der Schweizerischen Volkschule*, 3 Vols.; and Scherer's *Die Pestalozzische Pädagogik*.

The biographical facts are based chiefly upon Morf, *Zur Biographie Pestalozzis*, 4 Vols., and the biography prefixed to Mann's edition of Pestalozzi's selected works (*Ausgewählte Werke*, 4 Vols.). In these chapters I have tried especially to bring out the gradual development of Pestalozzi's pedagogical views.

References to Pestalozzi's own writings, which are of course the final authority for his opinions, are chiefly to Mann's edition (referred to in the notes as M.). Writings not included in this edition are usually quoted from Seyffarth's collected edition of the whole of Pestalozzi's works. In the case of *How Gertrude Teaches her Children*, references are to the paragraphs as numbered in Mann's edition.

The bibliographical appendix is based upon Volume XXV. of the *Monumenta Germaniae Pedagogica*, which gives an almost exhaustive bibliography of the literature of the subject. How vast that is may be judged from the fact that the bibliography contains nearly eight hundred pages! It is, however, not quite complete; for example the "Letters on Early Education," written by Pestalozzi to J. R. Greaves and published in English in 1827, are not included.

I have to thank several friends who have helped me in various ways, and, in particular, my wife and Mr. J. A. Lumsden; the latter was good enough to read through the book in MS.

If this little book does no more than indicate the extent of Pestalozzi's work and the far-seeing character of many of his intuitions, and if it thus serves to pave the way for more exhaustive and original treatment of the subject, it will perhaps have justified its existence. So wide are the topics which Pestalozzi from time to time touched upon, that the study of his work ought to form a good introduction to the scientific study of educational problems. History suggests that this should be so. Pestalozzi was the forerunner of Herbart, and Herbart's own work is easier to understand when Pestalozzi's more concrete point of view is properly appreciated. In this respect, too, the book may perhaps be useful.

J. A. G.

TABLE OF CONTENTS.

PAGE

PREFACE v

CHAPTER I.

GENERAL HISTORICAL INTRODUCTION . . . 1

The Renaissance and the Reformation—Luther and Melancthon—The Jesuit schools—Bacon and the modern scientific spirit—Comenius—The German Enlightenment—Pietism and the Realschule—Rousseau—The Philanthropinists—Frederic the Great and Maria Theresa—Rochow—Social unrest—Widespread interest in Education—Schools in Switzerland.

CHAPTER II.

PESTALOZZI'S LIFE: (1) ZÜRICH AND NEUHOF . . 16

Early environment and education—Zürich a famous literary centre—Pestalozzi's teachers—His interest in social reform—Political unrest in Switzerland—The Helvetic Society—*Der Erinnerer*—The ideal life—Neuhof becomes an industrial school—*The Ephemerides*—Letters on the education of poor children—Pestalozzi's failure—*Evening Hours of a Hermit*, Pestalozzi's educational creed—*Leonard and Gertrude*—Gertrude's educational practice—Glüphi's school—*Christopher and Elizabeth—Das Schweizerblatt*—Fichte and Pestalozzi—*Researches into the Course of Nature in the Development of the Human Race*—Family troubles and their consequences.

PAGE

CHAPTER III.

PESTALOZZI'S LIFE: (2) STANZ, BURGDORF AND
YVERDUN 40

Revolution in Switzerland—Pestalozzi in Stanz—Pedagogical development—Pestalozzi in Burgdorf—Appreciation
of his work—Krusi and Appenzell orphans—Pestalozzi and
Krusi in partnership—Room for experiments wanted—Independent Institute opened—Tobler and Buss—*How Gertrude
Teaches her Children*—Herbart and Pestalozzi—Dean Ith's Report—Institute nationalised for purpose of training teachers
and supplying school books—*Elementary Books*—Pestalozzi
has to leave Burgdorf—Work there reviewed—Münchenbüchsee—*Views and Experiences*—Yverdun Institute opened—
Wochenschrift—Report to Parents—Brilliant success of
Institute—Seeds of decay—Niederer and Schmid—*Swansong* and *Life's Destiny*—Return of Schmid—Successful issue
of collected edition of Pestalozzi's works—New Year's Address 1818—Clendy—Defence of Yverdun—Training of
teachers—Institute closed—Last publications—Death.

CHAPTER IV.

THE AIM OF EDUCATION 69

Pestalozzi's interest in Social Reform—Education as a
social factor—Relation of individual to social whole—Social
progress depends on individual progress—Germ of humanity
in every individual—Education concerned with its development—Human powers are threefold in character—Educator's problem is however one, and not threefold—Description
of man who is all that his neighbours think a man should be
—Disposition and Efficiency—Faith and Love—Freedom of
Will—Home and School—Education and Life—Types of
schools—Whilst general aims of education must always be
kept in mind, the individual in his concrete limitations must
always be taken account of.

CHAPTER V.

INTELLECTUAL EDUCATION 82

Axioms of general application—Definite ideas the aim of intellectual Education—Definition and Description, Clear Ideas—Distinct Ideas—The three elementary means—Mistakes in Pestalozzi's analysis of distinct ideas and their origin —Progress from vague to definite ideas—Abstraction—Carefully organised sensory experience the basis of mental progress—Things, real experiences, not words—When does child advance from distinct to definite ideas?—Linguistic development in race and individual—No temporal line of demarcation between periods of development — Was Pestalozzi a formalist? — His verbalism and his views as to the function of words—What the "Elementary Method" means—*The Mother's Book*—The "heuristic" method—Graduation of subject-matter of instruction—Law of Physical Distance and Doctrine of Apperception—History as a school subject—How individual differences in aptitude and rate of development were provided for at Yverdun.

CHAPTER VI.

PRACTICAL EDUCATION 113

Knowledge without practical power a curse—What Pestalozzi means by practical power—Psychological pre-conditions shown in his treatment of Drawing—Physiological conditions, "nerve tact"—Mechanical exercises not educational—The "psychological moment"—ABC of practical power—General training to precede special, *e.g.*, drawing before writing— Niederer's Drill—Physical training at Yverdun—Physical training and practical requirements of life—Home duties the best of all practical training—Varying needs of different individuals, *e.g.*, peasant and artisan, rich and poor—Progress in practical skill—Various school dexterities—Singing— Manual training.

CHAPTER VII.

MORAL EDUCATION 131

The key to Pestalozzi's system—Three stages of development: natural, social, moral—The psychological foundations
of morality—Law of " natural " nearness—Intercourse with
mother—Ideas of God—Transition to school—Home and
School—Stanz and Yverdun—Study of individuality—ABC
of moral feelings—Moral environment—Basis of idea of law
—Purity of feeling—Will—Discipline of practical and intellectual exercise—Motives—Interest in work itself—Relation
to teacher—Moral frame of mind comes through actual
experience—Words are dangerous—Formulation of moral
law does not belong to school age.

CHAPTER VIII.

THE SCIENCE OF EDUCATION AND THE TRAINING OF
     TEACHERS 151

The aims and spirit of Pestalozzi's research—His doctrines
to be regarded as a whole—The relation of the science of
education to the teacher—One goal but many ways of reaching it—Compromises often necessary in practice—Pestalozzi's relation to contemporary philosophy—His avowed
purpose was to rely entirely upon the facts of experience in
building up his science—A persistent experimenter—Necessity for experiment on a wide scale—Danger of too hastily
adopting results—Teachers must learn to experiment—Steri-
lity of a fixed method—Experimental schools—Kant's views
thereon—Collection of other people's results—Co-ordination of
results—Point at which Pestalozzi breaks down.

PAGE

CHAPTER IX.

THE INFLUENCE OF PESTALOZZI . . . 165

The social motive in education—Widespread interest in the social teachings of Leonard and Gertrude—Early disciples of Pestalozzi in Prussia : Gruner, Herbart—Prussian educational activity stimulated by Fichte—Humboldt, Nicolovius and Süvern—Pestalozzian doctrine penetrates Prussia through and through—Herbart and Pestalozzi—Fröbel—A new literature of education — Niemeyer — Harnisch —Diesterweg — Teachers' Seminaries—Pestalozzianism in the schools changes curriculum, spirit and method—School and Life—Teaching of Geography, Arithmetic, Drawing, the Mother Tongue, Reading and Music –Influence in England.

APPENDIX I.

PESTALOZZI'S STANZ LETTER 184

APPENDIX II.

(1) SOYAUX' ACCOUNT OF THE WORK AT BURGDORF 199
(2) VULLIEMIN'S ACCOUNT OF YVERDUN . . . 206

APPENDIX III.

PESTALOZZI'S CHIEF EDUCATIONAL WRITINGS, WITH SHORT ANALYSIS OF THE CONTENTS OF THOSE NOT SUFFICIENTLY DEALT WITH IN THE TEXT . 210

CHAPTER 1.

GENERAL HISTORICAL INTRODUCTION.

Renaissance and Reformation—Verbalism of the Schools.

THE History of Education in Western Europe, as a branch of the History of Culture in general, takes a new point of departure in the Renaissance of the fourteenth and fifteenth centuries. Great intellectual movements necessarily bring in their train changes in the theory and practice of education, and, reversing the point of view, one may regard the schools as an index to the penetrative effect of new ideas and new modes of thought which from time to time stir the current of intellectual life.

The spirit of the Renaissance spread over the whole of Western Europe, and after a long and bitter struggle, the traditional teaching of the higher schools and Universities had to adapt itself to more modern needs. The invention of printing told in favour of the new learning. The limitations which ecclesiastical tradition and the relative scarcity of books had put upon the schools were removed ; Greek studies were revived, and the prose of Cicero, as a basis for the study of Latin, replaced the rhymed grammars which had for centuries held sway in the schools.

But whilst the Renaissance did much to stimulate the intellectual life of the higher schools, its effect upon education as a whole was not immediately and entirely good. The events of this period, for example, caused the severance of what, for convenience, we call primary and secondary education. A gulf was fixed between them which few countries have even yet been able to bridge satisfactorily. With all its faults, the Church of the Middle Ages was distinctly a democratic institution; it always kept open the way for the clever boy from the parish song school which provided the priest with his choir boys, to the school of the monastery or cathedral, which introduced him more or less completely to the whole range of Mediaeval studies embraced in the seven Liberal Arts: thence he might beg his way to one or other of the great teaching corporations which developed in the thirteenth and fourteenth centuries, and there pursue more specialised studies at the feet of the greatest masters.

Universities and grammar schools were so altered in character by the Renaissance, that the direct line of continuity from the primary school upwards was broken. The boy who knew his psalter by heart and could intone the responses accurately was not in a position to take up the new studies of the grammar schools, which were becoming less and less subordinate to mere ecclesiastical needs. The storm in the sea of education carried higher schools right away and left the elementary schools stranded.

Then came the Reformation. For Luther the elementary school was the centre of interest. It followed from his doctrine of direct individual responsibility in the matter of salvation that every person should be put in a position to find out for himself his duty to God. Every one must be able to read the Bible, and, since the language of the people was not the language of the accepted version, he himself translated the Bible into the vulgar tongue. But in his view, the function of the school was just as narrow as in Mediaeval times. It was as much the handmaid of the Church as ever, although his conception was a much more embracing one. All children, boys and girls, must learn to read the Bible and must be taught the catechism, which Luther himself had written for them—"the spelling book of their religion," as he called it,—and the state should use its powers to compel neglectful parents to send their children to school.

Learning for its own sake did not appeal to Luther; his violence and anti-humanistic attitude threatened to detach the new learning entirely from the Reformation, as it had estranged Erasmus. In this respect the situation was saved by Luther's friend Melancthon, who was a scholar first, and then a reformer. Through him the modern German Gymnasium was established. That is to say, schools which were at once Protestant and Classical were founded over the whole of Germany. By publishing Greek and Latin grammars and other school books, as well as by advising upon the appointment of teachers, Melancthon contributed enormously to their success. As a counter stroke on the Roman Catholic side, a magnificent system of classical schools was organised by the Jesuits in the interests of the Church. In France, at least, these schools were unrivalled, and for two centuries they held the field of secondary education almost unchallenged.

The New Scientific Spirit — The "Enlightenment" — Pietism.

But what the Reformation had done for education in Central Europe was largely undone by the Thirty Years' War. At the same time, the ancient classical culture which now dominated the higher schools was being threatened in its turn by a new point of view, which refused to look upon the writings of the ancient Greeks as the ultimate source of wisdom. In truth, the New Learning had only substituted one authority for another, the philosophy of the Greeks and the literary form of Cicero for the dogma of the Church and the rhymed grammar of Alexander de Villa Dei. In 1620, Bacon published the *Novum Organum*, in which he gave expression to a growing revolt against the attitude of mind involved in the practice of the schools and universities. It was not in books but in experience that truth was to be found. All ideas which do not come from experience are "idols" which darken men's minds and conceal the true nature of things. Words themselves often blind us to the truth. Men must cease to quote Aristotle as the final authority. They must learn to read in Nature's book, which has many secrets to reveal.

Bold investigators had already challenged the truth of many traditional conceptions. The Ptolemaic theory of the universe itself was giving way before the calculations of the mathematicians and the observations of the astronomers. Bacon himself did not realise the force of his own words; he rejected the theory of Copernicus and doubted the use of the telescope while Galileo was making his startling discoveries. Yet he gave literary form to a widespread feeling that it was a vicious point of view which laid it down that everything knowable had been discovered by the ancient Greeks and was to be found in their books, and that, therefore, the best education a youth could have, was a literary education such as Erasmus would have approved, or rather, such as the Jesuits were giving in their schools.

The verbalists were attacked from another quarter. What Rabelais had said of the verbal sophistries of the scholastics, Montaigne said in politer language of the already degenerate word-teaching of the Humanists. At

the same time, Latin was still the language of the learned
world, and instruction in Latin was accepted as necessarily forming the central feature of the school curriculum.
We therefore find educational reformers giving expression
to the new ideas in improved methods of teaching Latin.
Things must be taught with words. When the words
have a genuine content they will be learned all the more
rapidly.

To make the doctrine applicable to early lessons in
Latin, Comenius published an illustrated Latin primer
(*Orbus Pictus*) in 1658, the forerunner of all our modern
instructive picture books for children. "There is nothing
in the intellect which has not found its way there through
the senses," was the guiding principle of the new school.
Comenius did much more to apply the new spirit and
above all, the new regard for nature to the whole problem
of education, than to write a first Latin book, but his
Great Didactic (1628), which is by far the most
exhaustive educational book written in the seventeenth
century, had little influence upon the practice of the
schools. The darkness of the period of the Thirty Years'
War (1618-1648) was too dense to be pierced by a treatise
upon education, however brilliant it might have been.
Amongst his contemporaries and for some generations later
the book was practically unknown.

The wonderful accomplishments of scientific research
had another effect, which in its turn involved the problem
of education. The human intellect had achieved such
triumphs that men began to look upon reason itself as the
final test of truth. The taint of intellectual arrogance
which characterises eighteenth century thought is in part
perhaps justified by the proud record of the seventeenth
—the century of Galileo, Kepler, Harvey, Descartes,
Pascal, Boyle, Newton, and Leibniz. Nature and Reason

were the watchwords which now guided men in every sphere of thought. What mankind as a whole believed, was natural, what was natural was reasonable. The two terms are scarcely to be distinguished.

Thus, almost side by side with the great strife of sects which followed the Thirty Years' War, there grew up a school which looked upon the externals of religion and the varying dogmas of churches as unreasonable in their very particularism, and which advocated a "natural" religion. Its creed was exhausted by belief in the existence of God, in the immortality of the soul, and in compensation for the ills of this world in the rewards of the next. These were doctrines universally held, and were, therefore, natural; that is to say they belonged to human nature, they were "inborn ideas" which were not to be gainsaid.

The application of the idea, Nature or Reason, to every sphere of human activity is the characteristic feature of eighteenth century German thought, of the German Enlightenment (*Aufklärung*) as it is usually called. The stimulus came from England (through France), and especially from the writings of Hobbes and Locke. We have seen the direction it took in religion : its ethics were founded upon the natural self-love of man, modified by his equally natural, though duly subordinate, if benevolent, interest in the welfare of others. It was "natural" to wish to make the best of this life, and both religion and ethics had a utilitarian *raison d'être*. Its treatment of political theory is especially characteristic of its arrogance and of its method.

Since what appealed to reason was true for these thinkers, they had no temptation to go outside their immediate environment in order to find out how things came to be what they were. The aim was to arrive at a reasonable theory which would connect the facts as they saw them, the civilisation of European States on the one hand, and the ill-understood barbarism of Africa on the other. The ideas of the state of nature and of the social contract, which were the bases of the political philosophy of Hobbes, Locke, and Rousseau, were invented and ingeniously adapted to explain the particular form of Government which the writer was concerned to condemn or to defend. The failure to realise the fact that historic development is in itself a natural phenomenon was one of the most conspicuous defects of the " Enlightenment."

The " Enlightenment " had considerable influence upon both the theory and the practice of education.

In the first place, its utilitarianism influenced a religious revival which was the natural reaction from the rigid insistence upon the dogmatic differences even amongst the various Protestant sects. This unbending orthodoxy attached more importance to forms of words than to inner convictions which find expression in conduct, and as a protest, first Spener in Frankfort-on-Maine, and then Francke (1663-1727) in Halle preached that religion was primarily a matter for the heart. The " Pietist " movement—a sort of continental Wesleyanism within the Lutheran Church —spread, and under Francke's leadership it took up the cause of education. Religion was to be the central theme, but the hearts of the children were to be touched. The school was to be, as it were, a continuous children's mission. More than half of the whole day in the primary school was given to religious instruction and religious exercises.

Francke's foundation at Halle embraced a free school for the poor, an orphan school, a school for the children of townspeople, a middle school, a higher school, a girls' high school, and a training college. The institution still exists, and is a conspicuous monument both to the man and the movement he initiated. The German *Realschule* also owes its origin to Pietism. The idea was first expressed in a project of Francke's to add to his many-sided work in Halle, another school in which the sons of country gentlemen and merchants who were not going to continue their studies at the University might learn subjects specially required for their future careers. *Non scholae sed vitae discendum* was the principle underlying Semler's plan for carrying out Francke's suggestion, in the sketch of which, published in 1708, the term *Realschule* was first used. "In this school the pupil shall be trained in those sciences which are indispensable to his daily life." It is the utilitarian idea of the " Enlightenment," grafted upon a movement at first strictly religious in character.

Rousseau and the Philanthropinists.

But the typical German schoolmasters of the " Enlightenment " were the Philanthropinists, who took their inspiration from Rousseau. In 1762, Rousseau published *Emile*, a book which, with all its faults, created an educational atmosphere in Western Europe such as would have favoured the temporary success of the wildest attempt to carry out a " natural " education as Rousseau conceived it. In words of passionate eloquence, he combined the ideas of Locke and Montaigne upon the education of a gentleman's son with his own views upon the rottenness of society and the banefulness of that culture in which his contemporaries took so much pride, and produced a scheme of "natural " education in which artifice itself becomes a cult.

Emile is an orphan to whose education a grown man of fine psychological insight is sacrificed for twenty-five years. He is removed from society altogether, and his tutor is his perpetual companion. He learns nothing until the psycho-logical moment arrives; that is to say until he feels an actual need. Books especially are "taboo." There is to be no hurry. If the boy is left alone all will go well. Emile is not to learn either to read or to write until he is twelve, and then only if he wishes to. Things are his teachers, and he is to feel no other limitation and no other stimulus than that due to things. He does not learn science, he discovers it. Of course, the tutor's business is to create the environment, to see that the boy is placed in educative situations and to be ready to help him out of difficulties when he is appealed to. In this "natural" way the boy's physical, intellectual, and moral development are furthered until he is ready to play a man's part in a society of which he knows nothing. The general attitude of the book towards educational practices current at the time was that everything was wrong, and, to be right, it was only necessary to do the opposite of what the world generally was doing.

In spite of its follies and contradictions, *Emile* was an epoch-making book. It interested people in education as they had never been interested before, and it taught people to look at the problem from the child's point of view, to regard the perfection of the child *qua* child as the important thing at the moment, instead of trying to make of him an epitome of the adult. Although it was only the upper classes who, in Rousseau's view, needed education, the book inspired men whose "Enlightened" views extended to the whole of humanity, men who saw no reason why the intellectual freedom which eighteenth century thought had won should not be the common property of all.

The Philanthropinists—or Friends of Humanity—deliberately set themselves to apply the principles of the

"Enlightenment" to education. Basedow, who had attracted attention by his work as a teacher in Altona, issued an appeal for funds to publish his ideas upon education. The book was to take the form of an elementary introduction to knowledge in general for use in the home. Subscriptions poured in, and what was later republished as *The Elementary Work*, appeared ; it was a collection of all the knowledge necessary to the education of youth from the beginning up to the fifteenth year for the use of parents, teachers, and private tutors. Along with it, a folio containing a hundred copper-plate illustrations was issued.

In 1774, under the patronage of the Prince, he opened at Dessau a school which he called the Philanthropin, because it was to educate "friends of humanity." The educational experiment attracted wide attention in Germany, and although, after various vicissitudes, the school had to be closed in 1793, it had really accomplished a great work ; numerous schools were founded on the Dessau model both in Germany and Switzerland. In their educational theory and practice, the followers of Basedow applied the principles of the "Enlightenment" directly to the school. They abolished the catechism ; and whilst they tolerated all forms of religion, they taught in the school only the principles of natural religion ; they appealed here, as in all subjects of instruction, to reason.

Throughout, their aims were strictly utilitarian. Naturally they taught best those subjects which would be useful to the children in later life. To enable the children to learn quickly, they adopted Rousseau's principle of teaching through things. Object teaching was carried on almost to the point of absurdity. Discipline was gentle. In order to provide their boys with the necessary motive power, they relied chiefly on an elaborate system of numerical marks which brought valued privileges to the

successful. They attached great importance to soundness of body, and, to that end, they encouraged open air
life, active out-door games, excursions into the woods,
bathing, fencing, etc.

The Social Motive in Education.

But the Philanthropinists did not touch the problem of
popular education. The spirit of the "Enlightenment" made
itself felt, however, upon a number of ruling princes, and
conspicuously upon Frederic the Great and Maria Theresa.
The Prussian king gave up the barbarous idea that a
people were easy to govern in proportion to their ignorance,
and at his instance, the education law of 1763 was enacted
—a law which is still the basis of the Prussian school
system. Maria Theresa, having heard of the success of
Felbiger, an Augustinian, in reorganising the schools of a
Catholic province of Prussia, invited him to undertake a
similar work for the whole of Austria, after the suppression
of the Jesuits in 1773.

Not only Princes, but noblemen also occasionally took
an enlightened view of their functions. Chief amongst
these was Rochow in Prussia. He lived amongst his
people and realised their ignorance. By founding and
fostering schools, and by writing school books, he hoped to
improve their intellectual and moral condition. As a
whole, however, the nobility held aloof from such reforms
as were attempted, and the people themselves were not
really reached by these purely external influences. They
had not yet become conscious of themselves, and although
the educated classes took an academic interest in the
question of popular education, it was not until after the
battle of Jena (1806) that the people as a whole were prepared to listen attentively to a Fichte, and to set to work
seriously in the organisation of a national system of schools.

Long before that, however, the study of social problems had become a fashion. There were numerous societies and many journals devoted to the discussion of social and moral problems. Every centre of intellectual activity amused itself in this way. The organisation of prize competitions for essays upon set subjects was a favourite method of provoking interest.* Here and there, of course, deeper convictions and abler men combined to produce serious contributions to the subject. Amongst the best of such societies was the Helvetic Society in Zürich, and the *Ephemerides*, published by Iselin in Basel, was conspicuous amongst the serious journals of the time.

Position in Switzerland.

Education was, therefore, in the air in the latter half of the eighteenth century, and behind it was a new motive— philanthropy, the love of man. In Switzerland, which was of course closely connected with Rousseau, improvement in education was a leading feature of the programme for social reform. The political position of the Swiss peasantry, which was little to be distinguished from serfdom, prevented anything being done on a large scale. But some member, of the privileged classes attempted to follow in a smaller way Rochow's example and to improve the lot of their dependents—notably von Tscharnen, and Daniel Fellenberg. The former wrote a "Guide for Country School-masters" (1772), and important "Letters upon the Education of poor country children" in the *Ephemerides*. Lavater's "Christian Booklets for children" (1769), and Iselin's "Essay on the improvement of public education in a republican business town" (1779), are alike interesting

---

* Rousseau's earliest literary work was a competitive essay in which he maintained that human culture in all its forms was pernicious in its effects.

examples of the practical interest taken in education, and
are typical of the widespread influence of the Philanthropinists, to whose work and methods both men had given
their support.

In towns like Zürich, practical school reforms were
introduced, but the position of Switzerland as a whole
was exceedingly difficult. The loose confederation of
eighteen tiny sovereign and twenty-seven semi-independent
states was beset with the vices of parochialism, and until
the revolution of 1798, carried through at the point of
French bayonets, broke up the confederacy and established
a central executive, it was not possible to do anything for
education as a whole. The new government— the Swiss
Directory—only lasted from May 1799 to March 1803, but
under the lead of Stapfer, its Minister of Arts and Science,
who was unexpectedly called from his Professorship of
Philosophy and Philology at Berne to this office, a brave
attempt was made to put popular education on a sound
footing. How badly action was needed may be judged
from contemporary accounts. In Canton Zürich there
were some 350 country schools of which less than a hundred
had buildings of their own, and such buildings as there
were could not have been more unfit for their purpose.

"As one opens the door, an oppressive damp strikes one.
Packed in a dark corner sit our country's greatest treasure
—its youth; they are compelled to breathe the hot air
reeking with thick foul mist. The windows are never
cleaned, the room is never aired. The children are so
closely heaped together that it is impossible to get out
without climbing over the seats and tables." Most of the
schools were in private houses: "I keep school in my own
house, and have only one room for both my household and
the school. I receive no rent and no allowance for school
furniture," writes one of the masters. Occasionally the

schoolmaster had to hold school in different houses in turn. Schoolmasters were usually badly paid, and necessarily had to combine schoolkeeping with some other business.*

The art of keeping school was not therefore far advanced. The children's duty was to learn and the schoolmaster's duty to hear their lessons. Twice each "school meeting," he made the round of his pupils, each one of whom was learning his particular piece of work in his own way. Class teaching as we know it, was unheard of in the village school. The children learned to read, to say by heart the church catechism, selected portions of the Bible, and many prayers. Writing was usually only taught when parents particularly wished it, and even the elements of arithmetic were regarded by many schoolmasters as a luxury which they themselves could well nigh dispense with.

Of method in teaching, as we understand it, there was no thought. A child would come to school not knowing his alphabet. The teacher would show it to him in his book, say it to him once over pointing to the letters and tell him to sit down and learn it. In an hour-and-a-half he would come again to test him. This process would go on for many weeks, until finally the child could say it through and was ready to take the next step. Want of method, and ignorance on the part of the teacher were made up for by an abundant use of the rod. The children hated the school, and learned nothing there that could possibly help them to lead self-respecting lives.

It was in times like these that Pestalozzi came upon the scene. How much there was to be done for education we can in part realise by comparing our present elementary schools with the accounts just given. From Pestalozzi more than from any other man came the spirit which has

---

* *v. Morf,* Vol. I., pp. 18 ff.

enabled the great educational reforms of the nineteenth century to be carried through, but Pestalozzi was a child of his own age in so far at least as he gave expression to some of its leading motives; he did not in any sense create an enthusiasm for education. It was there waiting for some definite guidance, and this at least Pestalozzi helped to give. Above all, what was wanted at that time was a man who knew the people and their needs intimately, not from without, as a nobleman like Rochow or a king like Frederic the Great might know them, but from within; a man who had lived in their midst, who had suffered with them, and fathomed the depths of their moral and intellectual distress.

CHAPTER II.

LIFE OF PESTALOZZI.

I. ZÜRICH AND NEUHOF.

Early Environment and Education.

HEINRICH PESTALOZZI was born January 12th, 1746, in Zürich, where his family, together with other Italian Protestant refugees, had settled in the middle of the sixteenth century. His father was a surgeon and oculist of some repute when he died in his thirty-third year, Pestalozzi, the second of three children, being only five years old. The family means were so straightened, that it was only through the services of a devoted but quite uneducated woman, Babeli, that his mother was able to make both ends meet. His early life was spent in an atmosphere of loving self-sacrifice. Naturally sensitive in temperament, all the circumstances of that time were calculated to appeal to his feelings in the highest degree, and his father's early death deprived him of what might have been a strong correcting influence, and thus have spared him many of the troubles of his later life. Nevertheless his environment was the source of much that is most characteristic of his educational doctrine. As we shall see later, his "idea of elementary education," so far at least as it is concerned with moral and religious training, is an honourable monument to the home life which gave it birth. "It is at once the product of, and an expression of gratitude for, all that his mother and Babeli had been to him."

16

Physically always a weakling, Pestalozzi, the "mother's boy," in spite of intellectual gifts of a high order, did not shine at school. He was always the butt for his school-fellows' practical jokes, and he did not please his teachers, who saw no promise in a pupil who could neither spell correctly nor write legibly, and who, besides, had no head for arithmetic.

In the Gymnasium (*Collegium Humanitatis*) Pestalozzi found an environment more suited to his nature. The teachers there included men of almost European reputation. Through the teaching of Bodmer and Breitinger, Zürich shared with Leipzic the honour of being the centre of that new literary movement in Germany which, largely inspired by English models, finally destroyed the limitations which French classicism had placed upon poetic and dramatic effort. Bodmer had been one of the first to recognise the real merit of Klopstock's *Messias*. He saw in it the first great achievement of the new poetic ideals, and when Klopstock visited Zürich, he found there, especially in the younger men, keen literary interest and susceptibility, to which his presence in turn gave a powerful impulse.

He was followed there by Wieland and other celebrities, one of whom wrote: "Zürich is really an incomparable place, not only on account of its magnificent situation, which is quite unique, but also on account of the intellectually eminent men who are there. Whilst in great Berlin one would probably hardly meet more than three or four men of genius and taste, in tiny Zürich there are certainly twenty." Although Pestalozzi was only six years old at the time of these historical visits to Zürich, their influence had not died away when he was old enough to be affected by it.

Breitinger was Professor of Greek and Hebrew when

PEST.

Pestalozzi entered the Gymnasium. He regarded those languages as the chief source of wisdom for all times and all peoples, and he knew how to make his pupils look upon them from the same point of view. " He was the type of a good teacher," says Morf, and he was loved and honoured as a father by his pupils.

Bodmer taught history and politics. He conversed with his pupils rather than lectured to them. In the classroom, and on the walks he frequently took with his pupils, his intercourse inspired them with intense love of freedom and justice, and many famous citizens of Zürich owed both guidance and inspiration to him.

These teachers exerted a powerful influence upon their pupils, and particularly upon Pestalozzi's sensitive nature. He carried their ideals frequently into extremes of practice, They enjoined simplicity of life and the practice of bodily endurance and hardening. Pestalozzi became a vegetarian, and slept on the hard floor of his room without clothes and without covering, until outraged nature brought him back again into more reasonable ways. Ideals of freedom, moral, intellectual, and political were advanced as things worth living and fighting for. Pestalozzi, in the midst of a political struggle which at times threatened to bring him into serious trouble, whipped himself till he bled that he might be able to bear the pain of any punishment his ardour should bring upon him. Writing in his old age of his schooldays, whilst recognising the value of the intellectual stimulus he received, he tells us that the entire want of practical reference in the teaching tended to produce a dreamy idealism in the boys which made them unfit to deal with the concrete facts of life, but as little really great has been accomplished except by men who have devoted themselves to what others have called the wild dreams of unpractical idealists, perhaps we owe more to the training Pestalozzi received at the hands of his Zürich teachers than he himself could have realised.

Pestalozzi's interest in social and political questions was further fostered by his holiday visits to his grandfather, a devoted clergyman in Höngg, a village in the near neighbourhood of Zürich. He accompanied his grandfather in his visits to the school and the houses of his people. There he learnt to know at first hand the ills of the country peasantry. He saw how little the "ABC and Catechism schools" did for them, and he realised the disastrous consequences for both mind and body, that came from the general practice of sending little children as early as possible to the factories which were then springing up around Zürich. The ignorance of the people, their suffering, and their inability to help themselves made a deep impression upon his mind. Already the resolution to devote his life to helping them had taken shape in his mind. "Ever since my boyhood my heart has yearned to stop at its source, the wretchedness into which I saw the people had sunk."

His education was intended as a preparation for the ministry. As a clergyman, he expected to have abundant opportunity for carrying out his plans, but the circumstances of the time, coupled with his failure in his first sermon, led him to regard the law as offering perhaps the most direct means of effecting his purpose. But his youthful ardour for political justice, for truth and right, brought him into such acute conflict with the authorities, that he had to give up all hope of a public career.

Politics.

Political interest in Switzerland at the time, centred in the struggle between the citizens of Geneva and its ruling families. Although nominally a republic the government of the city was practically a hereditary oligarchy. During the greater part of the sixteenth century, the citizens had been chiefly engaged in the defence of the town from external attack, and during this time powers had been provisionally vested in leading families, which they continued to exercise after all danger from without had disappeared. So long as they remembered to what circumstances they owed their position, their administration was conciliatory and passed without challenge. But they gradually assumed further powers and began to look upon their privileged position as their sacred right.

Towards the end of the seventeenth century, the citizens ventured to question these privileges and to demand a share in the government of the city. In 1738, they secured the unconditional right to make representations to the Magistracy, but the events of 1762 showed how illusory this right was. In that year, the Genevan oligarchs, in imitation of the Parliament of Paris, condemned Rousseau's *Emile* and *Social Contract*, as dangerous to the State and the Christian religion, and sentence of imprisonment was passed upon the author. The citizens appealed against this judgment, and asked that it should be withdrawn, but the petition was refused, and the Magistracy claimed that any petition which they thought proper to refuse, *ipso facto* fell to the ground.

Naturally the people of Zürich watched this struggle very closely. The leading men of the town and the majority of the people looked with suspicion upon attempts to subvert existing institutions. But Bodmer and those whom he influenced felt differently. They took up the cause of the citizens of Geneva with the utmost warmth, and Bodmer founded the Helvetic Society (1765) in the hope of advancing the cause of freedom. The young

Pestalozzi was a particularly active member. Rousseau's teachings were a gospel to these patriots. Many tried to put them into practice. " It is wonderful how some of our best students have taken up the idea of becoming farmers. They have already gone to help with the harvest as a sort of apprenticeship, to see if they can endure the heat, the sweat, and the rain," wrote Bodmer in 1765. In the same year, the patriots founded a weekly newspaper, the *Erinnerer*, to which Pestalozzi was a frequent contributor.

As politics were forbidden to the journal, it was devoted to the discussion of social, educational, and moral questions. The political situation was not any easier, and the Zürich councillors were getting impatient with the active young members of the Helvetic Society who had brought to light several cases of official corruption, thereby making enemies on every hand. The decision to send troops to coerce the recalcitrant citizens of Geneva added greatly to the excitement, and Pestalozzi, as one of the most zealous of the patriots, was suspected of being an accessory to the escape of the author of a lampoon directed against the authorities. Although he was shown to be innocent, he was under arrest for three days, and the offended magistrates never forgave him for his part in these matters. As long as he lived he was a dangerous demagogue in their eyes.

The Farm at Neuhof.

Thus was destroyed any lingering hope that Pestalozzi may have had of following a legal career. His most intimate friend advised him to give up all thoughts of public life and to seek the quiet pleasures of a country calling. The example of his fellow students occurred to Pestalozzi. He decided to burn his manuscripts, and to become a farmer.

At that time, Tschisseli's agricultural success in the
Bernese Emmenthal had attracted widespread attention.
He had converted a large track of apparently worthless
land into a number of valuable farms, thereby establishing
the welfare of five villages.   Many people went to learn
his methods, Pestalozzi among them (1767).   After a
year with Tschisseli, Pestalozzi spent his small patrimony
in purchasing some fifteen acres of waste land in the
neighbourhood of Zürich.   He obtained the financial support of a Zürich banker, bought more land, and in 1769
married Anna Schulthess, the daughter of a well-to-do
merchant in the city.

He had already began to build a house on his newly
acquired but heavily mortgaged property.   He called it
" Neuhof," and when they made it their home, the " ideal
life " seemed at last to have begun for Pestalozzi.   But he
was unbusinesslike to the last degree, and misfortune
soon overtook him.   From the beginning, his enterprise
was doomed to failure.   The land he had bought was
quite unsuitable for his purpose.   He was cheated on
every hand, and his strenuous but ill-directed efforts could
not prevent the ruin which unfriendly comment was quick
to foresee.   Unfavourable but authoritative reports led the
banker to withdraw his support, and Pestalozzi, although
he was always unequal to business detail, endeavoured to
retrieve his position by adding a wool-spinning business
to that of the farm.   Naturally his difficulties increased,
debts accumulated, and ruin was imminent.   Family
friends had exhausted their patience and their means in
their endeavours to help him.   Some drastic change must
be made or he and his wife would have to leave their
home, endeared as it had been to them by the birth of
their son, whose education was Pestalozzi's only joy
during this anxious period.

The Industrial School at Neuhof—its Aims and its Failure.

It was the practice of the farmers of the neighbourhood to take orphan apprentices from the parish authorities. If sufficiently overworked and underfed, these poor children proved profitable to their masters, but the ultimate effect on the children themselves was disastrous in the extreme. Ignorant and entirely dependent upon others, they developed into hopelessly degraded men and women. Poor as Pestalozzi was himself, he and his wife had intellectual interests which helped them to bear the burden of poverty without personal degradation. He longed to be able to teach these people how to live self-respecting lives, and he conceived the plan of converting Neuhof into a school, in which the children of the very poor might be so trained physically, morally, and intellectually that they should look upon work as a means of self-help and as a source of personal freedom, rather than as a sign of their dependence and degradation.

In spite of opposition from his wife's family, the scheme matured and Pestalozzi ventured to publish it. A number of people were interested. Of these Iselin of Basel was the most important. As the editor of a periodical, the *Ephemerides*, which was devoted to social and economical questions, he was in a position to give wide publicity to Pestalozzi's schemes.

The idea was that Neuhof should become a self-supporting industrial school. In summer the children were to work in the fields, in winter they were to spin and weave. In the intervals, and even whilst engaged in handwork, they were to receive instruction in the elements of reading, writing, and arithmetic. By the help of subscriptions and of loans free of interest, the new foundation had a short period of

apparent prosperity, but Pestalozzi's old faults once again
brought him to the verge of ruin. Within a year, the
existence of the institution was endangered. An appeal
for public support brought much-needed help and renewed
the interest of Iselin, who, after satisfying himself as to
the value of Pestalozzi's work, published the appeal in his
journal. Its columns were further opened to Pestalozzi,
who contributed a series of letters on the education of the
poor, in which he set forth his ideals and frankly recounted
the lessons of his experience (1777).

These letters are important, as showing how definite,
even at this early period, were Pestalozzi's ideas upon the
education of poor children. At the outset, he lays it down
that " inasmuch as it is generally true that each generation
of mankind will exercise its powers chiefly in the same
circumstances, and in the face of the same limitations and
difficulties as its predecessors, it is most essential that
what we do for children in their learning time, should in no
way incapacitate them for the kind of life they may be
expected to lead later on. The most important application
of this general truth I find in the bringing up of the
children of the poor for the most difficult of all life's
callings—poverty."

" The poor must be trained to poverty." In such
state institutions as exist this fundamental principle
has been overlooked. They have left undeveloped in
the children just the qualities which poverty itself
would have brought out, and in consequence they are
really nothing less than " nurseries of men unaccustomed
to industry," and therefore quite unfit to endure the
mischances and limitations of poverty. Any school
for the training of the children of the poor must be
primarily an industrial school, and one only needs to see
the work done in their homes by children of six years of age,

steadily increasing in efficiency year by year, to realise the possibility of combining industrial and mental training.

Yet Pestalozzi is not blind to the higher aims of education, for he thinks it quite as possible to train character in an industrial school as in any other. The essential thing is earnestness of purpose. " By the heart alone can the heart be guided."

As for the physical side of education, he thinks an industrial school offers indisputable advantages. Three years' experience has convinced him that intelligently planned and lovingly directed industrial work has much less evil effect upon growth and stamina than is commonly thought ; indeed, he has seen many cases of children who, when taken out of the idle wretchedness in which they were pining away, have been restored to ruddy health and strength by steady work at the spinning wheel.

The practical difficulties and disappointments he had had to meet were in no way minimised. Experience had in part at least disillusioned him. Children hardened in bad habits are not readily amenable to kindly treatment. Their training is a long and painful process, not seldom ending in failure. They are often ungrateful, and parents frequently encourage their ingratitude, even inducing them to leave the school perhaps just when they are decently clad, on the plea that their benefactor is waxing rich upon the fruits of their children's involuntary labours.

The greatest difficulty of all is to develop a religious feeling in children who always have lived, and always will live, in the midst of evil. There is only one way, that of awakening in them a lively belief in God as One who requites in their proper measure both good and evil, and in Jesus as their Saviour. One must pray with them morning and evening, asking God to preserve their hearts in innocence.

Pestalozzi's first pedagogic venture was thus an attempt

to develop, in grossly neglected children, the elements of humanity, which his faith assured him existed even in the most degraded. To carry out his aim, he thought it worth while "to live for years like a beggar among beggars, in order to teach them to live like men." His successes were numerous enough to convince him, that human nature as a whole might be ennobled by the organisation of industry in the service of education. He believed that schools of this kind once started would become self-supporting, and even provide a surplus which might be applied to the foundation of new schools. A steadily increasing number of children might thus be rescued from the miseries which generations of oppression, poverty, and neglect had entailed.

Unfortunately, Pestalozzi was not the man to give practical effect to such an attractive scheme. Self-sacrificing devotion to lofty ideals, unless united with business capacity, could not bring permanent success to pioneer effort. Subscriptions could only postpone the day of reckoning. In 1779, the financial crisis came, the institution had to be closed, and had it not been for the help of friends, Pestalozzi and his family would have been homeless. Neuhof was saved to them.

They were, however, reduced to the bitterest poverty. His family connections abandoned him altogether, and most of those who had shown interest in his philanthropic schemes forsook him. Keenly as he felt his position, Pestalozzi grieved most for the cause which his failure had discredited.

"The Evening Hours of a Hermit."

His faith in his ideas was stronger than ever. "I had made a great effort, I had learned great truths, and gained invaluable experience. My conviction of the importance of

what was fundamental to my views and my confidence in
my work were never greater than at the moment in which
it had to all appearances completely broken down."

"If I had to live on bread and water for years, and to
work in the humblest cottage in order to attain my object,
I would laugh at any danger, and would be certain of
ultimate success, even in my greatest need. I will do a
work such as no man has yet done, one which shall have
the greatest possible results for the people."

Iselin and one or two others remained steadfast friends,
and the former suggested that he should continue the
pursuit of his object by writing. Ready to do anything
which would keep his family from starving, Pestalozzi
began what is generally called his period of literary activity,
by publishing anonymously in the *Ephemerides,* a series of
aphorisms entitled "The Evening Hours of a Hermit"
(1780). They were addressed to "the shepherds of the
people and the wise of the earth." Written in an hour
of the deepest gloom, they bear the impress of the moment
of their origin, yet in Raumer's words* they furnish "the
programme and key of Pestalozzi's pedagogical system, the
plan of a gifted architect who is convinced of the value of
the work which destiny has prevented him from carrying
out." Niederer† speaks of them as containing the earliest
outline statement of the whole range of Pestalozzian
principles.

The author of the aphorisms sees mankind vaguely yet
profoundly dissatisfied with life, the meaning and purpose
of which men do not understand. Those who might be
expected to help in this emergency can do nothing—Pastors
make no effort to understand the nature and the needs of
their flock. In his blindness and ignorance man gropes

* *Geschichte der Pädagogik,* Vol. II., p. 381.
† *Wochenschrift für Menschenbildung,* 1807, Nos. 13 and 14.

for the truth which is only to be found in the innermost
recesses of his own nature. The infant in arms, who is
learning lessons of love and gratitude, is on the way to it.
Faith and love are at its base, but the whole truth is unattainable. Man, however, does not need it. His range
of knowledge is limited. In the natural order, it begins
in his immediate neighbourhood and in his most intimate
relations. Thence it extends its bounds, but at each
expanse it directs itself again to the middle point, the
fructifying centre of truth. True human wisdom rests
firmly on the basis of an intimate knowledge of what lies
nearest to it, and on the trained capacity for dealing wisely
with its most immediate concerns.

All men need to be elevated to true wisdom, which is the
universal aim of education. To this general aim, all
specialised education must be subordinate. The way of
education is the way of nature, therefore the minds of
children should not be forced into distant fields, or be led
into the confusion of word teaching, before they have been
inclined toward truth and wisdom by first-hand acquaintance with the realities of their surroundings. First the
thing, then the word.

All man's native capacities and powers should have the
opportunity to develop by use and exercise. First in importance is the moral culture of the individual, for all
human wisdom rests on the power of a good heart,
obedient to truth. This is the universal aim of all education. But man is fundamentally social, and he must be
educated for society as well as for himself. In this
respect the family is pre-eminently the educative factor.
In it, all human relations are typified, and all man's finest
feelings are rooted. The child's love for his parents is the
starting place of his love for God, which is the source of
all restfulness in life ; and the rulers of men should see in

the relations of fathers to their children the noblest
pattern of their own obligations to their people.

As we shall see in later chapters, some of the most
characteristic of Pestalozzi's educational doctrines are here
suggested. But the aphorisms, or as they have been
called Pestalozzi's educational creed, attracted little
notice at the time.

" Leonard and Gertrude ": Gertrude's Home School.

His next literary venture was a more practical and
concrete contribution to the literature of social and educational reform. The holiday visits to his grandfather in
his boyhood and the last eleven years at Neuhof had
brought him into intimate contact with the poor. He had
himself suffered poverty, and as Pestalozzi said, only those
who have themselves been poor really know how the poor
live. These experiences were the source of the story,
Leonard and Gertrude, which was published in 1781 and
was afterwards extended to four volumes, the last three of
which were published in 1783, 1785, and 1787 respectively.

Pestalozzi knew the village life of his native country as
few of his contemporaries knew it, and in the first part of
Leonard and Gertrude he is concerned especially with
showing exactly the condition of affairs. In his simple
story he makes clear the far reaching effects of a corrupt
officialdom. Every household in the small community of
Bonnal suffers from the malicious influence of the man
who is at once the village innkeeper and the official representative of the landowner. The whole atmosphere is
contaminated, and the people are for the most part sunk in
degraded and depraved poverty. There is, however, one
exception, the household of his heroine, Gertrude, who is
the model wife and mother. She saves her husband,
Leonard, from the toils of the unscrupulous tavernkeeper,

and through her action Arner, the new squire, who is anxious to do his duty to his people, initiates reforms which ultimately lead to the dismissal of the arch offender.

In simple convincing pictures the household of Gertrude is described. Her talks with her children, their eager response and ready helpfulness in the work of the household, their little acts of self-sacrifice in their mutual devotion, extended under their mother's wise guidance to suffering neighbours, are all set forth so tenderly that one cannot help feeling that the pictures come from Pestalozzi's recollection of his own child life. Here we have in the concrete the doctrine which is characteristic of all Pestalozzi's teaching, that family life is the greatest of all educative factors, that the mother is God's appointed teacher, before whom all others sink into insignificance.

In the second book, the problem of education comes rather more prominently forward, and in this respect Gertrude's household is again the centre of interest. The squire, his friend Glüphi, and the parish clergyman are coming to the conclusion that permanent reform is not to be expected unless they begin with the children. They cannot do much for the parents, and they begin to realise that children entirely brought up in vicious home surroundings cannot be saved from moral ruin; on the other hand, if the home teaching is leavened with the Christian spirit, neither the incapacity of a schoolmaster nor the machinations of a wicked official could do serious harm.

In the third book, a cotton-spinner, Meyer, who has seen the mischievous influence of improvidence on the efficiency of his workpeople, suggests that reforms should be instituted which would bring the schools into the most intimate contact with the actual lives of the children, and stimulate

into activity the whole range of the children's powers
applied to the circumstances in which God had placed
them. The idea appeals to Arner and Glüphi, but how
is such a school to be set up? Meyer suggests that
Gertrude can tell them, for "she has worked wonders in
the education of her own children, and converted her
cotton-spinning room into a schoolroom which cannot be
surpassed. Each of her children is just what it should be
at its age."

They go to see her, and beg her to proceed as if no one
were there. The family has just finished breakfast. The
children help their mother to clear away, sit down to their
work, and begin to sing their morning hymn. Gertrude
reads a chapter from the Bible, the children repeat the
most striking passages after her until they know them by
heart. She explains nothing, as the lesson is meant for
the heart, not for the head. The work is arranged
according to its difficulty. The little ones who cannot
spin, pick over the cotton and take out the dirty pieces.
They are not hurried into reading and writing; the first
thing is to teach them to speak. With an old A B C book
they learn to pronounce the whole series of possible German syllables, but Gertrude attached greater importance
to actual conversation.

It is what they *do* together that is really educative.
" Except spinning, sewing, and the other household arts
of which she is a master, Gertrude knows little beyond the
beginnings of drawing and writing, and nothing at all of
what may be called technical education. Yet she contrives
to lay the broad foundations for such an education. The
children can measure exactly with their eyes; their hands
are steady, their imagination is exercised upon their Bible
stories, and their feeling for the beautiful, since it rested
on their lively belief in God, was lofty and sound. The

life of their wise and pious mother, in the fullness and loftiness of its truth passed over wholly into theirs."

She counted with them how many steps it took to cross the room, how many panes there were in the window, how many fingers they had, the number of threads they were spinning ; she taught them the bases of measurement by exercises in the sensory appreciation of long and short, narrow and wide, pointed and blunt, round and angular, and as they prepared their meals, or made the fire, or helped to carry the water and the wood, she made them realise the action of fire, of water, of air, of wind, of smoke, the difference between water standing in the tub and running in the brook, the various forms it took as ice, rain, hail, etc., its influence in dissolving the salt and in putting out fire. She never took them one step further than they could advance from their own observation, and in whatever they did, they were made to feel conscious of their own power and anxious to bring it into action.

" Leonard and Gertrude ": The Village School in Bonnal.

The result of the visit was that Glüphi decided to become a schoolmaster in Bonnal, and to try to introduce into the school the spirit and methods of Gertrude. He realised that whilst the child believed thoroughly in his parents, he did not at once put faith in his schoolmaster. The latter must, therefore, approach him in the parental method and manner, and make the child feel that the schoolmaster, like his parents, was most concerned to make him an independent personality, an end best reached by thinking more of what the child could do than of how much he knew. Current objections to popular education arose from wrong views as to what such an education should provide. Merely to remove ignorance was not to educate men. It was an incomplete view of the problem.

Above all, it failed to appreciate the necessity of taking into account the actual situation of each individual child.

The fourth book continues the account of reforms in Bonnal. Gertrude gives Glüphi much good advice. " It is useful and right that the children should get knowledge and be taught to do things at school, but it is not in these points that home education is especially wanting; the most important thing is that they should become something that is good and right, and the many-sidedness of the school in respect of stimulus and guidance is its great advantage over the home—that view of its functions the schoolmaster should especially keep in mind. The children should acquire the habit of doing right, and an unshakeable determination to maintain it."

Of course there are times of difficulty, and the villagers themselves often seem hopelessly inaccessible to higher ideas. Gertrude, however, never loses faith. " A man may live for a time without faith and love, without intelligence, and in absolute idleness ; but his capacity for love, for intelligence, and for work never dies altogether. And if that is true of a single man, it is even truer of a whole village." The schoolmaster, in particular, is discouraged, but Gertrude urges him to think more of the children and less of himself. He makes many mistakes in spite of his high-minded efforts, and at one time seems to be losing his influence with the children entirely.

A chance visit from the cotton spinner teaches him a fruitful lesson. The visitor tells the children a Bible story in their own home language, and at once finds access to their hearts. Little incidents of this kind teach him to study the children themselves, their peculiarities of speech, their ways of thought, their individual dispositions, and gradually his mistaken view that they were incorrigible, disappeared, and progress from that moment is rapid.

PEST.

The school approximates more and more to the home ideal. " When this does not happen," says the author, " the school is rather a forcing house, in which the children are bent to this or that form, than an institution which aims at the free and harmonious unfolding of the whole range of human powers and capacities." Hitherto, although the squire has sent complete equipment for practical work, on Gertrude's advice, Glüphi has refrained from using it. First, he must win the children's confidence and love. Bible talks, Bible reading, and genuine interest in their personal concerns finally bring success. Then a capable woman is added to the staff, the spinning wheels are brought in, and actual hand work becomes the central feature of the school machinery.

Important as practical training is, Glüphi always makes it subordinate to character training. He had abandoned the empty verbalism of catechism teaching current in those days, and substituted for it the simplest religious teaching, which centred in God's love for his children, combined with the habit of diligent work and kindly action. Work is a prime instrument in moral education in the Bonnal school. In the same way, intellectual education is directed to the support of the moral ideal. " The head should be as bright and clear within as the silent moon in the heavens." Children are not born muddle-headed, and Glüphi tries to preserve their native clearness by insisting on their seeing accurately, and hearing properly; he educates them to willing effort by exercising their powers of calm attention, and by refraining from burdening their memories with meaningless words.

In this respect, Glüphi's teaching methods illustrate another characteristically Pestalozzian principle. As we shall see later, Pestalozzi looked upon accurate observation as the fundamental requirement in the acquisition of knowledge. Glüphi teaches through the senses, he takes care that his children see and hear rightly, not merely in order that they may remember more easily, but because "the habit of accurate observation is the first step to practical wisdom."

Later in his life Pestalozzi planned a fifth and a sixth volume, but the MS. of the fifth was lost on its way to Paris, and the sixth was probably never written. The first volume he had called "a book for the people," the later volumes he regarded as written for the educated. Morf sums up the contents of the four volumes in the words: "Glüphi takes Gertrude's household as a model for his school, and in the course of its history he approaches more and more closely to her proceedings. The parish clergyman brings his cure of souls into harmonious relation with Gertrude's home life and Glüphi's school efforts, and the work of these three persons in the house, the school, and the Church is helped on by Arner, who brings to their aid the highest powers of the state, and these four primary institutions of mankind, working in harmony, give rise to a true education for and a nobler life amongst the people. The middle point is the home; its influence extends over into the school, and finally brings about a new life in the whole village. State, Church and School work with the family towards a common end, but all learn from the mother, in whom centres the highest activity, because she follows simply nature's voice and the dictates of a heart educated only through Faith and Love."

The first volume proved a great success, but its author's object was not attained. People liked the story, but nothing further came of it. He wrote *Christopher and Elizabeth*, a series of evening conversations, in which the sources of the evils in village life are more directly and pointedly insisted upon. The book was published in 1782.

Its didactic tone was not calculated to bring it into favour with the readers for whom it was intended. The same year saw the beginning and end of a weekly newspaper, the *Schweizerblatt*, under Pestalozzi's editorship.

The later volumes of *Leonard and Gertrude* were less successful than the first. The circle of readers grew less with each new part. His style is not in itself attractive, and only those who were keenly alive to social needs and dangers, philanthropists, and the more thoughtful members of the governing classes took the trouble to wade through the prolixities of the later volumes. Readers of this class were too few to make the books a source of profit to Pestalozzi, but he was brought by their means into direct contact with many men of power and influence. His correspondents were numerous ; amongst them were German, Italian, and Austrian ministers of the highest rank, who wrote to him for advice upon social questions which were forcing themselves upon the anxious attention of their governments.

Of the readers of *Leonard and Gertrude*, probably nobody owed more to it than Fellenberg, with whom Pestalozzi was later in his life to have many, not always pleasant dealings. Fellenberg himself said, " The book made a deep impression upon me, and every time I read it, I was more and more convinced of its truth, and it was in an access of deep feeling caused by reading it that I vowed to my mother that I would devote my life to the poor and forsaken children."*

Meeting with Fichte : " The Enquiries into the Course of Nature," etc.

A visit to his sister in Leipzic at this time was made memorable to Pestalozzi from the fact that he met Goethe,

* *V.* Mon. Germ. Ped., xxv., p. 58.

Wieland, and Herder there. On his return to Neuhof
(1793) he met Fichte, whose *Addresses to the German Nation*
(1807-8) kindled German enthusiasm for education as the
one means of national salvation. Fichte saw in Pestalozzi's
principles the key to the solution of the educational problem, and at his suggestion Pestalozzi set himself to write
a philosophical account of his views upon human nature
and the problem of its development. After three years'
hard work he published (1797) *Enquiries into the
Course of Nature in the development of the Human Race.*
Although to those who have Pestalozzi's whole career
before them the book is distinctly interesting, one cannot
be surprised that it found few readers at the time of its
publication. As he himself sorrowfully admits in the
edition of 1821, "scarcely any one had noticed the book,
although it had been before the public for more than
twenty years."* Its interest for us lies in the fact
that, on the one hand, we see in it how his fundamental
principles are related to the philosophical thought of the
time, and, on the other hand, we find in it a general account
of the ethical basis of Pestalozzi's pedagogy.

These "Enquiries" were the last product of his eighteen
years of literary work. During the greater part of
this time Pestalozzi and his family suffered many priva-
tions. His wife was now a chronic invalid, and only the
help of a faithful servant who established the most rigid
economy in the household, enabled the family to hold
together. To add to his troubles, his only son returned
home from his apprenticeship in Basel in a delicate state of
health.

His cup of sorrow was full to overflowing. Not one of
his many undertakings during the thirty years of his
married life had prospered. Yet it is to this period of trial

* *V.* pp. 131-134.

that the world owes the Pestalozzi to whom it finally gave ear. When he had taken his young wife to Neuhof his thoughts had been naturally turned to the provision of a comfortable home, in which he might enjoy with his family those rural pleasures which his friend had advised him to seek, the life which his youthful contemporaries at the high school had idealised as the happiest and most natural man could lead. As a greyhaired man of fifty, his bitter experiences had long ago convinced him of the vanity of pursuing purely external objects. His only wish now was for an opportunity of carrying through a plan which had little connection with his own worldly prosperity. The idea of reforming the education of the children of the poor had now become the dream of his life.

He had begun his active life full of enthusiasm for Rousseau's ideas. He had christened his only son *Jacques*, out of admiration for the author of *Emile*, in the literal inspiration of which he was almost a believer. But at Neuhof, Pestalozzi learned to distinguish the letter from the spirit of Rousseau's teaching, "to reconcile the kernel of truth they contained with the facts of life, and to see in that kernel the secret of an education which should build up the strength of the people." At Neuhof too he learned to know the people as they knew one another. He had suffered with them. What this had taught him we may read in *Leonard and Gertrude*. Intimate acquaintance with the most degraded of men had convinced him that the germ of good is not completely choked in any man, and that it only needed favourable environment to bring it to life. He had made a noble effort to bring the children of the lowest classes out of their surroundings and to solve the problem of their education. His failure only proved to him that the task was too great for private effort, that the resources of the state were required if reform on a large scale was to be attempted.   Finally, the events of the time convinced him that the duty of the state was not ended when it had abolished serfdom, that indeed the step would be a dangerous one unless it were associated with schemes for educating the people.

CHAPTER III.

LIFE OF PESTALOZZI.

II.   STANZ, BURGDORF AND YVERDUN.

Work in Stanz.

UNDER circumstances of the kind detailed in the preceding chapter, Pestalozzi decided to change his calling once again. He would give up literature and become a schoolmaster. He drew up a plan for a school on the lines he favoured, that is to say a school in which instruction and education centred round industrial training.

The political changes which were taking place (1798) seemed favourable. Stapfer, the Minister of Arts and Sciences in the newly constituted government, was an enlightened man, who as a professor in Berne had already shown the keenest interest in the subject of popular education. Pestalozzi's scheme won his approval, and at his instance the National Executive adopted it, and voted money for the purpose. Delay, however, ensued owing to difficulties in providing a suitable site, and in the meantime Pestalozzi was asked to take charge of a government newspaper, the *Helvetisches Volksblatt*, by means of which it was hoped that the new constitution might win the good will of the people, who in many districts looked upon it rather as a tyrannous infliction than as the guardian of a newly acquired freedom.

40

The political unrest was strongest in the Nidwald canton where it was fanned by the Capucin monks. It became serious enough to call for action on the part of the French, who had called the new government into being. The province was invaded by French troops and the unhappy villagers were treated with ruthless harshness. The little town of Stanz was reduced to ashes, and so many children were destitute that the Government decided to provide a home for them. On December 5th, 1798, they asked Pestalozzi to take charge of it, under the general oversight of two specially appointed commissioners. On the 7th he went to Stanz. He says, "I went gladly, for I hoped to offer these innocent little ones some compensation for the loss they had sustained, and to find in their wretchedness a basis for their gratitude. In my zeal to put my hands to the task which had been the great dream of my life, I should have been ready to begin even in the highest Alps and without fire and water, so to speak, had I only been allowed."

The outbuildings of the Ursuline Convent at Stanz were to be transformed into an orphanage, but little had been done when Pestalozzi arrived. The need, however, was pressing. In spite of unspeakable difficulties, he decided to receive a number of the now importunate little ones on the 14th of January. They were in a dreadful condition, both of body and mind. For more than four months they had lived as homeless beggars. Only a genuine Christian love such as glowed in Pestalozzi's heart, a love which saw a brother in the most abandoned of men, could have devoted itself to the task of raising them out of the slough of their existence under such circumstances as Pestalozzi did. He was all in all to the children: master, servant, father, guardian, sick-nurse, and teacher. There was only one room available. His only assistant was a housekeeper.

His exertions were almost superhuman. He was the first to rise and the last to go to bed, and even in bed he would continue to teach his children. He had no school materials. Nature and the children's daily needs were the only "tools" available. His difficulties were increased by the attitude of the surrounding people, who looked on him as the instrument of a hated government, and a heretic to boot who was endangering the souls of the children. All his old Neuhof troubles were repeated. His neighbours hindered and slandered him; some of his pupils betrayed him, though most of these were quick to find out the friend they had in him.

As at Neuhof, his aim was to combine instruction and industry, but he no longer looked on the produce of the children's labours as a possible source of revenue. School handwork was now rather a means of training physical dexterity, promoting bodily efficiency and mutual helpfulness. He had not in any case the equipment for giving instruction in manual work; but there seems also to have been a change in his point of view. His pedagogy was broadening. On the intellectual side, he sought primarily to cultivate the fundamental activities of the mind—" the powers of attention, observation, and memory, which must precede the art of judgment and must be well established before the latter is exercised. Only in this way can the judgment be preserved from the superficiality which comes from the facile fluency induced by its premature exercise— a facility which is always more fatal to the progress of humanity than the ignorance of simple people of good sense."

Whatever the children learned they had to learn thoroughly, and the cleverer children were employed in teaching the rest.* In circumstances of this sort there

* *V.* Appendix I.

arose in his mind the idea that there must be a simple and universal method of instruction, by means of which any mother might teach her own children effectively, and that if this could be found the schools would no longer need to trouble about the earliest elements.

His greatest anxiety was to win the hearts of the children; he felt that it was only by gaining their loyal and loving goodwill that he could ever hope to transform his wild pupils into attentive, well-disposed, and obedient children. He tried to make them feel like brothers and sisters, each one of whom had an interest in and duties towards the others. In the family atmosphere the feelings of love, gratitude, and unselfish regard for others might develop, thereby constituting the bedrock of the higher life to which he wished to lead his children. He trusted to this much more than to lessons in morality, for he felt that abstract generalisations were quite unsuited to his purpose.*

It is also worthy of note that the unpractical Pestalozzi discovered the "school slate" during his five months at Stanz.

His work at Stanz, however, was soon over. In June, the French army, having been severely defeated by the Austrians, once again approached Stanz. They needed every available building for their exhausted troops. The school had to be broken up. Short as the time had been, Pestalozzi's success had been almost miraculous. "Even before the spring sun had melted the snows from our mountains, my children were no longer recognisable." The men deputed to watch his work had at first generously acknowledged its value, though at a later stage, misunderstanding its nature, they were estranged because Pestalozzi

---

* *V.* Appendix I.

had been unable to accept advice and suggestions which they offered. Troubles of this kind, the continued hostility of the people, and the unremitting exertions the work itself had entailed, were proving too much for Pestalozzi. He was breaking down under the strain. For him the needs of the French army proved a blessing in disguise. He left Stanz to recruit in Gurnigel, a favourite Alpine health resort, hoping to return to his work restored in health when the buildings were free. He was not permitted to go back.

Of course his giving up furnished fresh opportunity for criticism and calumny. Even his friends said "Yes, for five months he may pose as a worker, but in the sixth it is no go." Or they would tell him frankly, "It would be ridiculous to expect a man to do something reasonable at fifty because he wrote something sensible at thirty." Yet in those five months Pestalozzi had done work which can never be forgotten, for his orphan school at Stanz is " the cradle of the modern elementary school. Over it rises the silent glory of a martyrdom which needs no legendary adornment for its exaltation."*

Burgdorf : What Pestalozzi had learned in Stanz.

On his recovery, to the astonishment of his critics, he showed that he had not abandoned his purpose. Through the good offices of Stapfer, work was found for him at Burgdorf, where an old friend of Pestalozzi (Fischer) had already gone to set up one of the cantonal training colleges for teachers, which Stapfer had planned as an essential part of his scheme for educational reform. From the point of view of his own development and of his constructive work, this, his third period of educational

---

* Schenkel: *Pestalozzi und dessen Bedeutung für seine und unsere Zeit,* p. 29. Mann, I., p. lxxii.

activity, is perhaps the most important. He was to receive a small quarterly salary, to have apartments in the castle, and to teach in the lowest school in the town—the school to which the children of non-burgesses were sent—conducted by one Dysli, a shoemaker, in his own house.

Pestalozzi had now a very definite aim before him. As already suggested, his experiences in Stanz had somewhat changed the direction of his outlook and effort. At Neuhof he was living with beggar children in order to teach them to live like men. They were all the poorest of the poor, and would probably remain so. Yet they were human, and might be taught to lead independent, self-respecting lives, *if properly trained for poverty.* A poor man need not be degraded by his narrow means to the level of a beast. To prove the truth of this conviction may be said to have been Pestalozzi's prime motive. At Stanz the children were poor indeed, but not all of them had always been so, and some might reasonably expect to return to the comfortable standard of life into which they were born. The type of pupil was, therefore, much more varied. The children's powers were not all deadened by bad home and school discipline.

He allowed this variety of capacity and of individuality to find free expression, and as he watched his children he saw the truth as he had never seen it before, that *human powers develop of themselves and in accordance with law.* The problem of the teacher, therefore, was to understand the nature of this development in order to know how to guide and further it. This problem he set himself to solve, and especially to find the point from which development began.

He was now interested in a wider question than that of the education of poor children, and although he was not long enough in Stanz to advance far towards its solution,

he learned some definite practical lessons there, which bore
fruit at Burgdorf. He tells us that "he learned the
importance of stopping over the beginnings . . . and,
as never before, the relation of the first steps in every
kind of knowledge to its complete outline." He saw in
the unschooled ignorance of his pupils "a power of
sensory apprehension and a firm grasp of that which
reached them through their senses, such as our A B C
puppets had never dreamt of." He learned the natural
relation of book knowledge to real knowledge, and the
drawbacks of a one-sided adherence to the former, which
means the absolute reliance upon words which are only
sound and noise when there is nothing behind them. "I
saw how this may actually hinder observation and prevent
a real understanding of the objects immediately about
us."*

In matters of pure practice, he tells us that he was
obliged to instruct the children without help, he learned
the art of teaching many together, and since his voice
was his only means of teaching, the idea of making the
children draw, write, or spin, at the same time as they
learned, occurred to him. The confusion of the repeating
crowd led him to feel the need of rhythmic utterance, a
practice which seemed to him greatly to increase the force
of the impression made by repeating the lesson.

Successful work in Burgdorf School.

He began his work at Burgdorf possessed of greater
technical skill, and having a clearer idea of what he
wanted to do than he had ever had before; but his
novelties were not pleasing to the cobbler schoolmaster.
Even Stapfer's influence had failed to obtain work for

---

* *How Gertrude Teaches her Children*, Letter 1.

Pestalozzi in one of the upper schools of the town to which the burgesses sent their children. Instead of learning the catechism, the children were repeating some A B C rubbish after their new teacher, and were frivolously wasting time over drawing. If this man was to experiment with the children, let him do it in the burghers' school. The parents could not fail to be attracted by this last argument, and they declined to allow their little ones to be experimented upon.

But this check did not prove serious. One or two faithful and influential friends obtained leave for him to teach in the lowest school of the upper town. The children were from five to eight years old. " I felt that I was really most fortunate, yet I was at first very shy. Every moment I feared they would turn me out of my schoolroom. I was, therefore, more nervous than usual, and when I think of the fire and the life of my first hours at Stanz, by means of which I built, as it were, a magic temple, and then of the nervousness with which at Burgdorf I bowed myself under the yoke as a matter of business, I can hardly understand how the same man could do both."

In spite of his trepidation and the irksomeness of the school discipline, " not free from pedantry and pretension," he continued his investigations and experiments with the same untiring enthusiasm and the same want of method as in Stanz. He was seeking the highways of education and instruction, and in the midst of dusty school duties, which began at eight in the morning and ended at seven in the evening, he was constantly lighting upon facts which indicated the existence of law in the processes by which our minds pick up and retain impressions from the outer world. A chance suggestion from an interested friend, *Vous voulez mécaniser l'éducation*, revealed to Pestalozzi the true nature of his

purpose.   As he did not know much French, he understood
the words to mean that he was " seeking the means of bringing education and instruction into psychologically ordered
sequence, and taking the words in this sense they threw
a flood of light upon his whole endeavour."   Hitherto,
" vague but vivid feeling " had been his guide ; now for
the first time he saw clearly the true nature of the path
which he was trying to follow.

Although in the course of his school work he could not always
be true to the principles he was gradually formulating, we
know that he did his duty faithfully, from the point of view
of the school authorities, for after a special enquiry and a
careful examination, his little pupils were found to have
made extraordinary progress under the novel treatment.
The report stated that "in eight months he had not only
taught children of five and six years of age to read perfectly,
but that the best among them could already write and
draw well, and had made progress in arithmetic.   He had
also succeeded in awaking amongst them all a taste for
history, natural history, geography, and geometry, and
future masters would be greatly assisted by the foundations he had laid."   They further remarked upon the
simplicity of his methods, which were such as "even an
intelligent servant might apply in the midst of her household duties."   The " School Board " congratulated their
new teacher, and showed their confidence in him by promoting him to a mastership in the second boys' school of
the town, where, with renewed zeal, he continued his pedagogical experiments (May, 1800).

Krusi Taken into Partnership.

One of the men most interested in Pestalozzi's work at
this time was, of course, Fischer, who not only proved himself a wise and sympathetic critic, but was the means of

introducing to him the man who became his first fellow-worker.

A number of orphans from the distressed province of Appenzell were, at Fischer's instance, to be provided for by charitable Burgdorf people. Fischer wanted a young man to bring the children to Burgdorf. He looked for one who wished to become a schoolmaster and to be trained for the work. Krusi was recommended to him. He had already had some practical teaching experience, and although almost wholly uneducated, he had an open mind, and considerable insight into child nature. In January (1800) the children arrived, and with them Krusi. Fischer did not remain long in Burgdorf after Krusi's arrival. His plans for a training college had not prospered. A month or two later he died from typhoid fever, but not before he had consented to a suggestion that Pestalozzi and Krusi should unite their forces. The former could hardly have found a better partner. Krusi had in a high degree what Pestalozzi had not, the art of the practical schoolmaster. He was also intelligent and modest enough to submit himself entirely to the intellectual lead of Pestalozzi.

In some respects, however, the combination added to Pestalozzi's difficulties. It brought a new element into the school in which differences of age had already proved a hindrance, both to collective work, and to the continuance of his researches. The worrying demands of anxious parents naturally increased when these pupils, for the most part of a very different type, were brought into the school. As freedom was absolutely essential to the work he had at heart, he approached the state authorities with a plan for an independent institute, in which he might follow his own course without external interference. With the help of Stapfer, his idea was approved by the National Executive, and a grant-in-aid was voted. Not satisfied with this,

Stapfer founded, in June 1800, a Society of the Friends of Education, for the express purpose of winning support for Pestalozzi in the country. In order further to justify themselves, the Society sent a commission to Burgdorf to enquire into Pestalozzi's work. In anticipation of their visit, he prepared an account of his principles and processes that they might know what exactly to look for.* The visitors were delighted, and transmitted a most favourable report to the government.

Encouraged by this double success, Pestalozzi decided to open his " Educational Institute for the Children of the Middle Classes " at once (October, 1800). In the following summer, through the good offices of Krusi, further assistance was forthcoming.

" How Gertrude Teaches her Children."

Two men, Tobler and Buss, joined their fortunes to that of the Institute. " With these three colleagues, Pestalozzi set himself to the task of establishing the practical consequences of his fundamental doctrines and of systematising his methods. At the same time he was working at a more elaborate statement of the ideas which were now taking definite form within him." The book, *How Gertrude Teaches her Children*, appeared in 1801, and for the second time Pestalozzi succeeded in attracting the attention of a wide circle of readers.

The book, which has profoundly affected subsequent opinion and practice in education, takes the form of fourteen letters to Pestalozzi's friend Gessner, a bookseller in Berne. In the first three he sketches the circumstances which brought himself, Krusi, Tobler, and Buss to the

* A translation of this appears in *How Gertrude Teaches Her Children*, Sonnenschein, pp.199-211. It was largely incorporated in Letters 4 and 5 of the same book.

work : in letters four to eleven he states the results of his reflections and of his experience in the sphere of instruction on the purely intellectual side. The twelfth letter discusses practical education, the education of the physical rather than intellectual powers, whilst the last two are concerned with the questions of moral and religious training.

As we shall treat in detail of its contents later, it will suffice now to say that Pestalozzi's purpose was to show that by reducing knowledge to its elements, and by constructing a series of psychologically ordered exercises, even an uneducated mother might be put in a position to fulfil the duty which nature intended should be hers—the education of her children. This was his reason for adopting the somewhat curious title which pointed back to Gertrude, the model mother of Pestalozzi's creation. Educationally, it is by far the most important of his writings. "It will remain for all time a corner stone in the vast educational structure which the nineteenth century has raised," not because it fulfilled its purpose in respect of the mothers, but because it established principles of education applicable equally to the school and the family.

Once again Pestalozzi had achieved a literary success, and visitors from all parts of Switzerland and Germany came to see the school in which his ideas were being worked out. There had been a steady stream of interested visitors for some time before the book appeared. In 1799, whilst Pestalozzi was still in the A B C school of Fräulein Stahli, a young German who was then a private tutor in a Swiss family had been to see what it was in Pestalozzi's practice that made the higher Swiss educational authorities put so much faith in him. This was Herbart,[*]

* *V.* also pp. 169-171.

who some years later succeeded to the Professorship of Philosophy at Königsberg, and who was to become the most
philosophical of all the exponents of educational theory.
He has himself expressed his indebtedness to Pestalozzi,
whose subsequent career he followed with close attention,
taking a leading part in spreading Pestalozzian principles
throughout Germany.

The number of pupils in the Institute increased, but in
one important sense this was not pleasing to Pestalozzi.
He had secured his independence, but he was a step
farther away from the great desire of his heart—that of
doing something for the children of the poor. He took as
many poor children as he could manage to keep, but he
saw no means of reaching the masses, except that of training teachers for the work. He had, of course, already
students, philanthropically-minded men who saw the
national need and were eager to find the remedy, but this
was not enough. He approached members of the Government who had shown interest in the work, and at their
instance a special commission was sent to examine into
the affairs and conduct of the Institution, and to report
upon the best means of utilising its services in the
interests of the public. The report of the two commissioners, of whom Dean Ith was the chief, gives an
interesting picture of Pestalozzi's work.

Dean Ith's Report.

After explaining Pestalozzi's principles, the report says
of the actual work : " There is no trace of memory drill.
Everything which the child learns is the result of his own
observation, of his own experience. He learns nothing
which he does not understand, he understands everything
which he learns. In the lower classes the chief exercises
deal with observation and naming. The boys are led to

notice first the objects in the room, then they go over the whole house, observing and naming everything. When this source is exhausted they are taken into the garden, into the fields, and the woods, gradually accumulating a large stock of mental pictures and names. The children are then led to notice the objects in greater detail, their situation and the relations of their parts, their permanent and changeable qualities, the qualities that are general and those that are peculiar to them, their influence, their function, and their destiny. Thus they pass from simple to complex ideas, from mental images and names to judgments, descriptions, conclusions—in one word, to the definite and intelligent use of language. They understand what they say, and they say what they understand."

For dogmatic religious instruction in the upper classes Pestalozzi employs a Protestant and a Roman Catholic clergyman, who give instruction to the children of their own communion; in the lower classes, child religion, not theology, is aimed at. The object is to stimulate and educate the moral feelings. To that end the whole life of the school as well as the instruction is religiously organised. Morning and evening prayers are specially adapted to the events of the day, and private talks with the boys do much to strengthen the impressions made by experience. Corporal punishment is rare. "It must not be thought that this moral atmosphere comes from fear or from the strictness of discipline." The rod is almost unknown. It is only used in the solitary cases where sensory excesses must be frightened away by sensory pains.

Many visitors had been struck by the uncleanliness of the institute and its general appearance of poverty. The report says, "As to the latter, I am not exactly in a position to deny it. But one must remember that the

Institute is essentially organised for the children of the poor, that it is not yet two years old, that it was started with absolutely no help or credit, and that nearly one-sixth of the pupils live at the cost of the Institute. To make matters still more difficult, school fees are always three months in arrear. They must, therefore, live from hand to mouth in the truest sense of the words, and this credit system, combined with frequent short payments at the end of the quarter, is one of the reasons why the institution has already several times been nearly ruined. At least 10 per cent. of the income is lost in this way. Surely the head of the foundation ought to be praised rather than reproached in respect of this poverty.

" As to cleanliness, I have noticed nothing which, under the circumstances of the Institute, could be easily avoided. My arrival at eight o'clock in the morning was quite un-expected, but I found everything in order; the dormitories and beds were clean and well aired, the children were combed and washed; their clothes varied of course according to their circumstances; the table was abundantly pro-vided in respect of quantity; as to quality there was obvious frugality, but teachers and children shared alike. For breakfast they have soup, for supper soup and vege-tables, for dinner, besides soup and vegetables, a small portion of meat and wine, and between dinner and supper a little fruit."

Accepting the report of the commissioners, the Govern-ment decided to transform Pestalozzi's foundation into a national institution. The staff were to receive fixed salaries, provision was made for twelve "students of the method," and sums of money were voted for the publication of the various school exercises which Dean Ith had remarked upon, as text-books for wider use. By this means, Pestalozzi was enabled to issue the three elementary books : (1) *The A B C*

of Sense-Perception, or Lessons in the Observation of Form;
(2) *Lessons in the Observation of Number Relations,* and
(3) *The Mother's Book.* They were the work of the whole
school staff under the general superintendence of Pestalozzi.
The last of the three was received with special hostility, but
the most objectionable parts were really the work of Krusi.*

It was about this time that two notable additions were
made to Pestalozzi's staff : Schmid and Niederer, men
destined to play the chief part in his future career. Schmid
came as a poor pupil, but his abilities were so conspicuous
that he was invited later to become a member of the staff.
Niederer had been a minister. He was well educated, and
naturally philosophical in his interests. He joined the
institute at Pestalozzi's invitation in May 1803.

Political changes inspired by Napoleon were again
imminent in the little Swiss Republic. A great national
deputation was sent to Paris to interview the First Consul
on behalf of the nation. Pestalozzi, whose political interests
had always been keen and strong, was elected a member.
Before going he published a tract containing his views
upon the general principles which should guide political
effort. It is an interesting document, which exhibits in
brief the interconnection of his political, social, and educational work. Summing up his argument he says, " Our
legislature should have its attention chiefly directed to the
four following objects : (1) A suitable scheme of popular
education, with an organised system of higher and professional schools based thereon, (2) a sound judiciary, (3) a
good military system, (4) sound finance." His visit to
Paris gave him no pleasure. He may have had hopes of
drawing attention to his own particular objects, but
Napoleon was too busy to trouble about his A B C.

* An account of the contents of these books will be found in
Appendix III., pp. 213-217.

The deputation was ineffective; and the political changes brought disaster to Pestalozzi's Burgdorf foundation. The new government located in Berne had no interest in it. They questioned his right to the tenancy of the castle, and finally gave him notice to quit, on the plea that the rooms were wanted for their own officials. To save themselves in the eyes of their critics, the authorities offered him the disused buildings of an old monastery at Munchenbüchsee. Although he received numerous offers of hospitality for his Institute from other towns, he elected to accept the Government's offer, and in June 1804 Pestalozzi's connection with Burgdorf came to an end.

Pedagogical Development at Burgdorf.

The change cut him to the heart, for the place was endeared to him, both by the friendships he had formed and the work he had accomplished there. As already pointed out, he began to teach in the Burgdorf schools with a more clearly defined aim than he had had either at Neuhof or at Stanz. His motives were no less philanthropic, but whilst his interests had broadened, his experiments had been concentrated upon the solution of a particular problem. His object was the simplification of the means of early instruction, the reduction of the teaching process to a psychologically ordered form which should be so perfect, so simple, and so certain that, whilst it might be regarded as an instrument of precision, it might also be successfully operated even by ignorant teachers. It was to be useful especially to mothers, whose work would dispense with the necessity of schools for the very young, which were wrong in principle, because they tended to break up the most natural and therefore the most effective of all educational institutions—family life.

At Burgdorf, Pestalozzi established the principle that

observation is the absolute base of all our knowledge, that the child should therefore first be exercised in the sensory examination of objects; next he should be told their names and the names of their qualities. Prior to this second step, however, he should be trained in accurate articulation of sounds which would make the pronunciation of words easy to him. Practice in the use of speech should proceed step by step with observation. These steps should be graduated on the principle of uninterrupted continuity, and each word as it is learned should be put into a sentence and repeated after the teacher. This is the principle of *The Mother's Book*,* and the famous "Hole in the curtain" lessons, which Ramsauer describes, are another example of the principle in practice.

"The best lessons he gave us were the combined observation and speech exercises, especially those which centred in the curtains which were hung round the schoolroom walls. The curtains were very old and torn, and in front of these we often had to stand for two or three hours together, and say what we could of the shape, number, and position of the holes and of the figured pattern. What we saw and mentioned had then to be gathered up into longer and longer sentences. Thus he would ask one of the children, mentioning him by name, What do you see? Answer: 'A hole in the wall,' 'a tear in the curtain,' etc. Pestalozzi: 'Good, now say after me

I see a hole in the curtain.

I see a long hole in the curtain.

Behind the hole I see the wall.

Behind the long narrow hole I see the wall, etc., or

I see figures on the curtain.

I see black figures on the curtain.

I see round black figures on the curtain.

* *V.* p. 213

I see a rectangular yellow figure on the curtain.

Near the rectangular yellow figure I see a round black one, etc."*

In working at the "elementarising" of observation he conceived the idea of an "observation alphabet" (A B C der Anschauung), by the use of which children should be enabled to compare, measure and reproduce form accurately, and in endeavouring to "elementarise" arithmetic he saw its intimate connection with form, and alongside the "alphabet of observation" he worked at an "alphabet of number relations." Along with *The Mother's Book*, these exercises constituted the three elementary books which have already been mentioned, a more detailed account of which is given in Appendix III. Sound, form and number were in his view established as the "three elementary means" of instruction.

At Burgdorf, too, Pestalozzi definitely severed himself from the catechetical methods to which Campe, Salzmann, and other Philanthropinists pinned their faith—Socratic instruction as they called it. It was on this point that he differed most from Fischer, who, as a pupil of Salzmann, endeavoured to train Krusi on the Socratic lines. Of course, Pestalozzi was dealing with young children, and, as he said, "a child cannot give out what he has not yet taken in," "the time for learning is not the time for judgment." Krusi, an ignorant but earnest student, had stumbled absolutely before the methods which Fischer tried to teach him; he welcomed with great relief Pestalozzi's outspoken criticism of this Philanthropinistic development.

Pestalozzi's stay at Münchenbüchsee proved short. Unwisely, as it turned out, his colleagues induced him to enter into an agreement with an old acquaintance, Fellenberg,

---

* *Raumer*, Vol. ii., p. 336.

at that time the head of a great industrial school less than a mile away; the business management of Pestalozzi's school was to be taken over by Fellenberg, whose organising capacity might be expected to keep the institution on a sound business footing. But Pestalozzi soon found his position had become intolerable. A rupture was inevitable, and in October he left for Yverdun, where two old teachers of his had already established a school. The time at Münchenbüchsee had been mainly spent in drawing up a great prospectus of the Pestalozzi-Fellenberg institution. It is a long document of fifty pages which was very largely the work of Niederer. It is the first sign of his growing influence over Pestalozzi.

Thanks to a timely present from the King of Denmark, in return for kindness shown to two Danish students at Burgdorf, Pestalozzi was enabled to spend the next few months at Yverdun in quiet literary work. He wrote his *Views and Experiences relating to the idea of Elementary Education*, and entered into controversies with the Philanthropinists, who claimed priority in respect of all Pestalozzi's teachings. After long and frequently unpleasant negotiations with Fellenberg, it was finally decided to remove the whole establishment from Münchenbüchsee to Yverdun, the authorities of the latter place having expressed their readiness to house it in the castle.

Although Pestalozzi was now on the point of entering upon the most brilliant of his practical successes, as a matter of fact his work as an investigator was practically finished at Burgdorf. His later writings are in the main based upon his experimental work there and his experiences at Stanz. In some respects these later writings, influenced as they were by Niederer, are less trustworthy accounts of his views than the Gessner Letters. Niederer became the mouthpiece of his master to such a degree that some not unimportant misunderstandings have arisen in respect of Pestalozzi's opinions.

Yverdun Institute.

The household was reunited in July 1805. A period of astonishing prosperity began. Pupils came to the lakeside village from all parts of Europe, and many governments, attacted by the social aspects of Pestalozzianism, sent young men to study "the method," with a view to its introduction into their own schools. In May 1807, a weekly newspaper, *Die Wochenschrift für Menschenbildung*, was started under Niederer's editorship. The most notable contents were (1) Niederer's scheme of physical education.* (2) The text of an address by Pestalozzi to the Society of Friends of Education at Lenzburg in 1809, "Concerning the Idea of Elementary Education." The text is both edited and annotated by Niederer, who often philosophises his master's principles almost out of recognition.† (3) Pestalozzi's Letter concerning his work in Stanz (Appendix I.); and (4) Report to Parents and to the Public upon the present work and condition of the Institute at Yverdun.

The Report to parents is a valuable document, inasmuch as it lays down the ideals which Pestalozzi and his staff held before them, and gives an authoritative account of the actual organisation of the school. Besides this, it expressly denies the equally damaging statements that the school was only for young boys of eight or ten, or that it was meant only for children of the higher classes who could afford to wait for the results of an exceedingly slow rate of progress. It tells us also that German and French were taught, and that boys who wished might learn Latin and Greek. The other subjects of the school were

* V. p. 119.   † V. p. 218.

geography, natural history (experimental and descriptive), history, literature, arithmetic, geometry, surveying, drawing, writing, and singing. The Report deals also in great detail with such questions as the moral and physical well-being of the boys, and the special pains taken to study the individuality of the pupils and to adapt the instruction thereto.

This Report was written in 1807, at the moment when Yverdun was at the height of its fame. Pestalozzi's fame had now spread over two continents. The man who had never been able to spell correctly, and who always readily owned to his friends that he spoiled whatever he put his hands to, had become the prophet of instruction and of education; the man who lived always in the present, and whose intellectual life, if we may accept Niederer's striking expression, had no history, was the inspiring personality of a movement of vast significance in the history of culture. The man who had scarcely been outside his own country had drawn to himself the astonished attention of the whole world, and the man who always complained of his absolute unfitness for a position of authority was the dominating force in a great movement and the object of a devotion which for his sake sought to make the "impossible possible."

The only explanation of such a series of contradictions is perhaps to be found in Pestalozzi's own expression: "I was taught as a child the holiness of meek and humble service, but now I have found out that even a grey-haired man may perform miracles if he too will minister to the lowly."

His devotion to the details of the work which he loved involved almost incredible hard work. With rare exceptions he was writing at two o'clock in the morning, and Ramsauer, who spent many years in the school, first as a pupil and later as a teacher, tells us that for years no member of the staff was in bed after three o'clock. The spirit of unity and brotherhood which reigned at Yverdun during the first four years was so perfect that, although the whole of the staff had free access to the school purse, nobody abused the trust. But even at the moment when their reputation was at its height, when their numbers were greatest and their material success was most striking, Pestalozzi's New Year address was most pessimistic in tone.

Canker of Disunion.

This was in 1808. He felt that the canker of disunion was silently growing amongst his colleagues. Although there was not yet an open conflict, different views as to policy were represented by Niederer and Schmid, and their differences of temperament were not such as made compromise possible. In the struggle for influence over Pestalozzi, Niederer gradually gained ground, and as his authority increased the Institution took a character further and further removed from the pattern of Burgdorf. The idea of making it a great international school naturally grew out of the fact that from the outset they had tried to serve two different linguistic areas—French and German. Whilst this increased the number of their pupils, it tended to destroy the unity of the educational arrangements. The curriculum was further broadened by the introduction of the classics and other subjects which the teachers were not really competent to undertake on Pestalozzian principles, and in regard to the treatment of which the master himself could not exercise an efficient oversight.

Pestalozzi felt that dangerous rocks were ahead, but Niederer's influence was too strong. Schmid, on the other hand, warmly opposed Niederer's policy, and outside critics were quick to see what looked like pretentiousness in the educational programme. Even the visitors who came from all parts of Europe, and who were the outward and visible sign of the glory of the Institution, were a source of difficulty. They took up valuable time and exposed the teachers to the temptation to work primarily for show.

In 1809 and 1810 criticism was so vigorous that Niederer suggested the advisability of inviting the Government itself to appoint an impartial commission to examine into and report upon the conduct and efficiency of the Institution. Against the urgent remonstrances of Schmid, Pestalozzi adopted the suggestion, and in 1810 the state commissioners were appointed. Their report did full justice to the nobility of Pestalozzi's purpose and character, but while much was found worthy of praise in the teaching of individual members of the staff, the general tone adopted by the commissioners was unfriendly. On the whole, they took the view that what was good in the work was not new, and what was new was far from good. The effect of the report was, that although the National Assembly expressed by resolution the thanks of the fatherland to Pestalozzi, all hope of Yverdun becoming a state institution for the training of teachers was completely cut off.

Pestalozzi felt strongly that justice had not been done to his Institute. A long-drawn-out literary feud followed, and Schmid resigned his post. Neither the one nor the other proved advantageous to Pestalozzi's cause. Schmid, although not a highly educated man, was an excellent teacher of mathematics, an organiser and a man of business. Neither Niederer nor Pestalozzi had capacity in these directions, as they showed shortly after when they added to their responsibilities by opening a printing and bookselling business, which soon proved a source of serious loss. Financial embarrassment ensued, but with the help of friends the foundation held together without Schmid until 1815, when he consented to return.

During Schmid's absence Pestalozzi's literary activity
had not slackened, in spite of the business worries which
crippled finances entailed. He wrote his *Swansong* and his
Life's Destiny—the former a restatement of his educational
doctrines, the latter a review of his life work. These writings
ings were not published until 1826, when they appeared as
one book, under the title *Pestalozzi's Swansong.* In 1814
he also wrote a long article addressed " To the Innocent,
Serious, and Magnanimous of my Fatherland." It is an
interesting testimony to Pestalozzi's ceaseless care for the
people whom his school could not then touch. He com-
plains bitterly that Switzerland is lagging behind Prussia
in this matter. The foundations of national welfare are
everywhere alike ; salvation lies only in the education of
the children, but the children belong to the parents and
not to the state.

" The imperial greatness of England rests on the in-
violable sanctity of the home. Napoleon's worst act was
that of handing over the machinery of the schools of the
poor and of the localities to the rough management of the
state. May all the noble and the good unite against this
tendency to forget that the home is the chief agency in the
education of the moral, intellectual, and physical powers."
Of course, Pestalozzi is not protesting against the establishment of universal schools, but he did object to purely
central control, which by making the schools mere cogs in
the wheel of a great machine, destroyed their individuality,
and cut off their connection with the home life of the
children.

Last Years of the Institute.

Schmid's vigorous measures of reorganisation did not
bring peace. After the death, in 1815, of Pestalozzi's wife,
whose influence had done much to prevent an open breach,

the oldest of Pestalozzi's fellow-workers, Krusi, resigned. Niederer followed him in 1817. Completely overcome by all these troubles, Pestalozzi threw himself entirely into the hands of Schmid, who was successful in raising a sum of money for a collected edition of Pestalozzi's writings which yielded a net profit of £2,500.

The New Year's address of 1818 was naturally pitched in a triumphant key, and in his new ardour Pestalozzi made a further appeal for funds to establish an Institute in which his old work at Burgdorf should be continued. He wished to see educational research resumed on a more settled plan. There should be an institute devoted to the further simplification of the means of instruction, the compilation of text books in the various subjects of instruction suited to popular education, and the training of men and women teachers in the spirit of home education ; alongside such an institution he wished to establish one or more schools in which the results of the research might be put to the test of carefully supervised practical experience.

The money already raised he decided to devote to the education of the poor. He had twice previously made an attempt to open such a school at Yverdun, but circumstances prevented the successful accomplishment of his purpose. Schmid at first objected, but as Pestalozzi held to his purpose he gave way. The new school was opened at Clendy in the same year (1818), and once again sunshine came into Pestalozzi's life. He had already in the *Wochenschrift* described his ideal school for poor children, and Clendy was to be of this type; but Pestalozzi had lost his grip, and gave way to the request of the Englishman Greaves, who knew neither French nor German very well, that he should be allowed to try "the method" in giving English lessons to the Clendy children. Then French and Latin were added. There was reason, therefore, in Schmid's proposal that the

work should be done at Yverdun.   Pestalozzi agreed, and
in 1819 the reunion took place.

Some objections were taken by the town authorities to
the children of rich and poor, both boys and girls, being collected under one roof.   This provoked Pestalozzi's "A word
concerning the present position of my pedagogical work
and the organisation of my Institute," in which one
finds the dominant interest in his mind then was the
training of teachers,* a subject to which he returned
in an address, "Views upon industry, education, and
politics, with especial reference to our position in these
matters before and after the Revolution" (1822).   The
people possess powers given to them by God ; Christ teaches
that it is the duty of the rich to devote their property to
the poor ; they cannot do this better than by helping to
found institutions in which men and women shall study
the development of human nature and human powers and
the means of assisting in that development, with especial
regard to the circumstances of the children.

If one might attribute any special development of
Pestalozzi's pedagogy to his work at Yverdun, it would be
the idea of a liberal professional training for teachers ;
liberal, that is to say, as opposed to a merely mechanical
training in the employment of particular means, liberal as
differentiated from mastering a particular technique.   He
conceived the idea of a science of education, applicable as
such to the education of all classes, and he is chiefly concerned to establish institutions of a threefold character.   In
one branch, the science of education should be the subject of
research, in another, the results of this research should be
put to the test of prolonged practical experience, and in the
third branch, men and women who are to become teachers

* *V*. Chapter viii.

should be taught the principles of their profession and, at the same time, associated with the research and the practical applications carried out in the associated branches. One hardly need say that Pestalozzi's ideal has scarcely been realised even to the present day.

All this time he was doing his utmost to effect a reconciliation with Niederer and Krusi ; but Schmid was the stumbling block, and, instead of reconciliation, long and painful litigation embittered Pestalozzi's last years at Yverdun.

The affairs of the Institute were going from bad to worse, and finally in 1825 it had to be closed. Pestalozzi returned to his old home at Neuhof, and although all his hopes had been shattered, he took up his literary work again with great vigour. He published the *Swansong*, in which he passes in review the whole sum of his endeavour, and a new *Life's Destiny* in which he describes with some acerbity the circumstances which led to the destruction of his Institution at Burgdorf and Yverdun. He was very proud at this time of being elected president of a local national society for the year 1826, and delivered an address to the society on " The Fatherland and Education," in which he describes the services education might render to a non-industrial country like their own.

But troubles were crowding in upon him. His *Life's Destiny* provoked many bitter responses. Fellenberg and Niederer in particular wrote angrily about it, but worst of all was a lampoon by Biber, who had been one year at Yverdun—*Contribution to Pestalozzi's Biography*. The old man suffered terribly from these attacks, not so much on his own account, but because men were pouring scorn upon his work, upon things which to him were holy. He fell ill on the 15th of February 1827, and died at Brugg two days later. His last words were : " I forgive my enemies. May they now find peace to which I am going for ever." He was buried in the churchyard at Birr. In 1846 a monument was erected over his grave. One sentence thereon fittingly sums up Pestalozzi's life-long struggles—

Alles für andere; für sich nichts.

CHAPTER IV.

THE AIM OF EDUCATION.

Social Reform.

PESTALOZZI's whole life was spent, directly or indirectly, in the furtherance of one object—social amelioration. He was over fifty when serfdom was abolished in his native country, and he was one of the most ardent supporters of the new order of things inaugurated by the short-lived Swiss Directory (1798-1803). From his early youth he had felt that the condition of things which made the peasant of free Republican Switzerland as much a bondman as his brethren in Russia was intolerable. He welcomed heartily the constitutional changes which redressed this wrong. Philanthropic efforts which are usually directed to the relief of the wants of the very poor had always seemed to him rather to increase than to reduce the evils they were designed to meet. To his mind the fatal flaw in social work of this kind lay in the fact that it did not teach men to help themselves, but left them more dependent than ever. " The best service man can render to man is to teach him to help himself." " Man as a whole in his inner nature must be improved if the external circumstances of the poor are to be bettered."*

* Introduction to *Views and Experiences*, M. iii., 324.

Though political freedom was a step in the right direction, it could not do more than remove obstacles to a
general improvement in human nature. But mankind as a
whole has no virtue; virtue is essentially an individual
quality. The state is not virtuous; it can only make use
of the virtue of its individual members. This must first
be established. "Those who wish to make the community
virtuous and strong, before virtue and strength are
developed in the individual, may frequently lead the state
into wrong action, because they try to fix the external
forms of virtue and strength upon men without making
sure that the essence of the thing is theirs."*
Legal reforms at best only clear the way. Years before
he decided to make teaching his profession he had realised
that the true sources of human well-being lie within the
individual man, and that to develop these is one of the
prime needs of mankind.†

Keenly disappointed with the selfishness and nepotism of
the political leaders, whose clamour for change culminated
somewhat unexpectedly in the revolution, men to whom
"the purer doctrine of his early days was only noise and
words," he ceased to expect a good issue from " the tinkling
cymbals of civil truth," as beaten by the men of his time,
and decided to become a schoolmaster.

In his pedagogy, as in his politics, social reform was the
prime motive of Pestalozzi's work. It is only in the light
of this fact that we can obtain a true idea of his educational
theories. Around him he saw, on the one hand, ignorance,
poverty, and degradation ; on the other, a crowd of insincere
politicians whose rhetoric was empty and inconsequent,
because it did not spring from a first-hand acquaintance

---

* Letter to Nicolovius, 1809 (Rein, Art. *Pestalozzi*).
† *Evening Hours*, M. iii., 10.

with facts. Words void of real meaning were bandied about from man to man as if they were true coin. For the moment the position seemed hopeless. Here was wretchedness and misery in plenty, and in the face of it, abundance of talk concerning " the rights of man " and other formulae current at the time, high-sounding, but in their use hollow and unreal. What else could be expected when education, from top to bottom, dealt with nothing but words, grammatical or ecclesiastical formulae which did not touch in any way the real lives of those who learned them ? Education wrongly conceived was the source of much social mischief ; education rightly understood and rightly carried out was the only radical cure.

In this spirit, and " with full faith in the possibility of improving the human race," he turned his attention to educational reform. In so doing he was acting in strict conformity with the whole intellectual movement of the time. If the intellectual freedom which the " Enlightenment " had won was to be preserved, it must become the property of all classes. As we have already seen, education was in the air. In 1770 Iselin had written: "The problem of education is to teach men to be men, and this is the greatest service one generation can perform for another." "We have spelling schools, writing schools, catechism schools, but we need *men's* schools,"* wrote Pestalozzi. The elevation of humanity, the making of men, was the aim he set before himself. *Humanity* inspired his labours at Neuhof and Stanz, the same philanthropic motive gave zest and meaning to his indefatigable experiments at Burgdorf; never entirely obscured even during the brilliance of his Yverdun success, it reappeared almost in its original form at Clendy, and the last utterances of the old man on

* *How Gertrude Teaches her Children*, xii., **9.**

the brink of the grave testify to his undying interest in
the social aspect of his work.

Development of the Powers of the Individual.

But society is a great aggregate of individuals and the
elevation of the individual is the only means of elevating
the whole. Pestalozzi saw the elements of humanity in
every man, latent human powers instinct with life, awaiting
the opportunity to unfold. The inner impulse is already
there, education has merely to furnish the opportunity and
to offer guidance.* It is its business to bring out these
latent powers, to watch over the process of development,
to guide them towards that sum of qualities we usually
call manliness, of which perhaps the chief characteristic is
strength, moral and social efficiency. "The development
of human nature, the harmonious cultivation of its powers
and talents, and the promotion of manliness of life: this
is the aim of instruction." "One may have produced a
good tailor, a good shoemaker, or a good soldier, and yet
not have produced a man in the highest sense of the
word."† "He is not a man whose inner powers are
undeveloped."‡

To work on lines of this kind was not the way to win a
reputation as a successful schoolmaster. At Burgdorf,
Pestalozzi's results did not please parents accustomed to
measure their children's progress by the usual tests.
Where he strove to build up capacity, they found ignorance
of the A B C; where he tried to teach his pupils to think,
feel, and act rightly, they found them unacquainted with
the catechism. The opinions of Krusi and Fischer,
which are quoted in the first two letters of *How Gertrude*

* *Swansong*, M. iv., 184.
† *How Gertrude Teaches her Children*, x., 22.
‡ *Evening Hours*.

Teaches her Children, show that more enlightened observers understood Pestalozzi aright. " He wishes to increase intensively the mental powers of the children, not merely to enrich their minds by the addition of ideas " (Fischer). " He (Krusi) now saw that in everything I rather tried to develop the inner powers of the child than merely to produce detached results for each of my several activities."

Pestalozzi was quite conscious that he was departing from the traditional paths. "The schoolmaster of the past," he wrote, " had regard to the external rather than to the inner life, to the superficial rather than to the essential, to the immediate requirements of daily life rather than to those of the man himself." " The teacher usually finds his starting-point in his subject ; you, mother, will find it in your child. The teacher has a fixed form of instruction through which he puts the child ; you will subordinate the course to the child's needs, adapting it to him as you adapt yourself to his physical demands."* The difference is clear. One is education by addition from without; the other is education from within, an endeavour to bring to full maturity the child's own nature in its original God-given purity. Parental complaints did not disturb his plans ; he continued his efforts to find the one and only way—" the way of nature "—to the goal he had set before him—the development of the inner powers of the children.

Although in the Gessner letters Pestalozzi does not explicitly state what those " inner powers " are of which he speaks, it is still obvious that he had the classification in mind which is expressly given in the opening sentences

---

* Preface to *A B C der mat. Ansch. für Mütter.* (*Wochenschrift,* v. Rein, Art. *Pestalozzi.*)

of the *Swansong* as *intellectual* capacity (*Geisteskraft*),
practical capacity (*Kunstkraft*), and *moral* capacity (*Her-
zenskraft*), using the term moral to include *religious*,
connoting, that is to say, the attitude towards God which,
in Pestalozzi's view, is the only true basis of right living.
He treats of intellectual education in Letters IV.-XI.,
practical training in Letter XII., and ethical and religious
training in Letters XIII.-XIV. These three sides of
human nature, he tells us, develop each according to its
own unchangeable laws. That is why he deals separately
in this book with three sides of education, (1) intellectual,
(2) physical and technical, (3) moral.

Has the teacher, then, three independent processes to
watch over ? This was not Pestalozzi's view. He fully
recognised the necessity of some unifying principle. To
define education as the process of developing the "inner
powers" of the child, and to follow this up by an
enumeration of those powers without explaining their
mutual relationships, could give no guidance to the
teacher. If he is to pursue three independent aims, what
is to ensure his maintaining the proportions which will
secure the "harmony of the powers," which is at the same
time desired ? Although the point is not explicitly met in
How Gertrude Teaches her Children, it is clear in his later
writings that Pestalozzi felt the truth as put by Herbart.

Character (Morality), the Final Aim.

"If it is to be possible to think over thoroughly and
accurately and to carry out systematically the *business* of
education as a single whole, it must be previously possible
to comprehend the work of education likewise as a whole,"
i.e. to regard it as pursuing a single aim. Even in the
Gessner letters, however, Pestalozzi tells us there is a
"keystone to his system," and in the thirteenth letter he

gives more than a glimpse of its relation to the intellectual
and practical sides of our nature, with the development of
which he has been previously concerned. "Education and
instruction must be brought into harmony with the feelings of my inner nature, through the gradual development
of which my mind rises to the recognition and veneration
of the moral law."

Indeed, one cannot read *How Gertrude Teaches her
Children* without realising that Pestalozzi might have
defined the whole sum of his endeavour as seeking to
establish in the child a Christian disposition, resting on
the broad basis of a cultivation of the powers which are
essential to practical life. The point, however, does not
really arise in the book, chiefly because it is concerned
primarily with intellectual education—that was Pestalozzi's
chief interest at the time of its publication—and not with
a general discussion of educational aims.

In his later writings he approaches the question over and
over again. The most exhaustive discussion is in the *Swansong*, but the point is taken up with more or less fullness
in almost all his later utterances, probably in answer to
contemporary criticism, which was often pointed and sub-
stantial enough to need attention.

"The whole work of education and its *only* work may
be summed up in the concept Morality." "Morality is
universally acknowledged as the highest aim of humanity,
and consequently of education." These are Herbart's
words. He follows them ·up by an examination of the
concept of morality, expanding its usual acceptation, and
demonstrating its real possibility. This is an orderly and
a scientific procedure, but it is not Pestalozzi's method.
Instead of defining morality, he gives us the plain man's
answer to the question, "What is that man like who is as
all men should be?" This ideal man shows in all his

judgments, in all his counsel, in all his undertakings, a
sound and trained intelligence; a steadfast, strong,
benevolent heart that is capable of any exaltation and
effort; and such skill and patience in his actions as
ensure a successful issue to whatever he takes up.

One-sidedness in any direction is fatal. The man of
cultivated intelligence who has no sympathy with suffering,
the philanthropist who is ever ready to sacrifice himself in
pursuit of good work but is wanting in tact, the artist who
is pre-eminent in his own sphere but is unfriendly and
self-seeking—all alike fall below the plain man's ideal.*
To sum up this whole idea one may perhaps say, that
Pestalozzi's ideal man is one whose benevolent disposition
is guided by intellectual insight, and made effective by
practical acquaintance with affairs. *Disposition and
Efficiency* are the determining factors.

To look more closely at what is here called Disposition,
we find that Pestalozzi is quite definite in his view as to
the elements which determine its nature aright. They are
Faith and Love. "I regard all the powers of the intellect,
all the practical skill and insight which belong to my
nature, only as a means for the divine exaltation of my
heart to love. Man's improvement is for me only the
advance of the race towards Humanity, and the sole
eternal basis for such an advance is Love." Instruction in
itself no more develops love than it develops hate; it cannot, therefore, be the essence of education. "Education
proper to our nature leads to love, *not a blind, but a seeing
love*, in which our moral, intellectual, and practical powers
unite, thereby constituting our humanity."† "But true
Love can only come from true Faith."‡ "In Faith and

---

* *Views and Experiences*, Letter iv., M. iii., 331.
  † Address, 1809.   ‡ *Evening Hours.*

Love alone our powers begin, continue, and end the process of their development. They are thus the Alpha and Omega of a natural education to humanity."* In the atmosphere of family love, the love of God and of our fellow man develops. This gives the tone and direction to disposition, which, combined with efficiency, constitutes character.

Granted, however, that human nature is capable of modification by the atmosphere in which it matures, the question naturally arises as to whether or not human nature is entirely a creature of its environment, whether the individual man is no more responsible for his ultimate form than the plant which the gardener tends or neglects as suits his purpose, whether man is pre-determined or self-determined, whether or not the will is free. Pestalozzi takes up the question in his New Year's Address, 1818. "Love and Faith," he says, "as the basis of education, presuppose the lofty freedom of the Will as the organic centre of all man's powers, and this presupposition makes it absolutely essential to recognise the duty of exalting the Will, through Faith and Love, to unselfish devotion to the cause of truth and right, to the truth of God and to the rights of our brethren."

Freedom of will and a sense of duty are not incompatibles. "The child must be prepared for the ready and active performance of the whole circle of his duties towards God, towards his neighbours, and towards himself. He must be vigorously trained to such sustained effort and prolonged endurance as the performance of duty may in the future demand."† "The educator must aim at the unification of all human powers for the purpose of their final determination in the freedom of the human will, through

---

* *Swansong*, xiv., 136.   † Cp. *Leon. and Gert.*, iv., chs. 71, 72.

Faith and Love."* "The education of our intellectual powers must be subordinated to the higher laws of our will; in this way we shall rather confirm and increase the strength, perfection, and independence of those powers than endanger their justice and truth."†

We may, perhaps, now put Pestalozzi's position in the following way. Whilst he was always moved by philanthropic motives, and by the great social benefits he expected education to bring about, he regarded the problem of education as primarily an individual one. He saw in each individual the germ of that which we call humanity. Its distinguishing factors involve, on the one hand, a personality which is free and self-determined, yet susceptible to external influence and guidance, and on the other a complex of powers, physical, mental, and moral, which are capable of indefinite and progressive advance. Whilst these powers are co-equal in a quantitative sense, and demand an equal amount of attention from the teacher, who must above all things avoid one-sidedness, in a qualitative sense it is always the ethical element, touching as it does the personality, that is of first importance. Intellectual, moral, and physical education are not to stand side by side in isolated detachment, they are to react one upon the other, with a due subordination of the intellectual and physical to the moral, which through faith and love is the basis of human personality.

The Aim of Education is throughout individual and concrete.

The individual character of the problem of education as viewed by Pestalozzi comes out again in a matter upon which much discussion has been raised, viz., as to whether

---

* Address, 1818.   † Preface to Lenzburg Address.

or not all children should have the same initial education, no matter what their position and prospects may be. Pestalozzi's own views have been frequently misunderstood, largely through the influence of Niederer, who acted for so long as his interpreter, and frequently edited his writings before they went to the press.

There can be no doubt of Pestalozzi's views on this subject before he came under the influence of Niederer, as we see from the fact that the twelfth letter in *How Gertrude Teaches her Children* is written from the point of view of the children of the poorer classes. In the concrete, education must take into account the conditions of life from which the child springs, and in the midst of which the child will in all probability spend his whole life. This is another reason why the home should be his first school, and why later on the "teacher must weave his accessory work into that of the parents' as a weaver works a flower into a whole piece of cloth." His *Letters concerning the Education of Poor 'Country Children*, his *Evening Hours of a Hermit* urge the same point. *Pestalozzi will have every child educated, but his education shall be suited to the life he will probably lead.*

Writing from Paris, he says: "The one great essential in elementary education is the harmonious development of the powers, but in their use subordinated to the demands of the actual circumstances of man. The child of my method feels his power only in surroundings that are real to him. He is not puffed out with empty learned words which have no background in his experience." * And again in 1803, to Countess Schimmelmann: "No one does more harm to our universal aims than the dreamy universalists. . . . We must, therefore, always attach popular education firmly to the actual needs of the people. . .

* Cp. Morf, ii., 147 ff.

Every real elementary school in every place must be suited to the particular circumstance of its situation if it is to fulfil its mission."* In the Lenzburg address he says: "All the exercises, the whole complex of means which are employed in elementary education must aim at establishing connections between the child and the realities of his actual life."

To the end of his life he held this view, and in the *Swansong* he goes so far as to consider the types of school suited to the farm labourer, the artisan, and the merchant or man of letters. The kind of education suited to each grade of society must be determined by the circumstances, powers, and necessities that are common to it. As a matter of fact, he was mainly interested in the first two—the country school and the town school, the school for the peasant and the school for the artisan, who together constitute the great bulk of the people.

In the education suited to particular walks of life, the universal aim of all education is not, however, to be forgotten. To be happy and useful in his own sphere is the particular aim of every man, and the attainment of this aim should be furthered by his education. " Nevertheless, education for particular walks in life must be subordinated to the general aim of man's education."† Without neglecting in the smallest degree the demands of human nature in the unfolding of a child's divine powers, he must be so trained that he will feel himself happy and blessed within the limitations of his home surroundings, and that he will freely and eagerly seek to acquire such knowledge and skill as will enable him to make his position satisfactory and prosperous, in spite of its peculiar difficulties and worries.‡ " The neglect of this principle, and the

---

* Rein, Art. *Pestalozzi*. † *Evening Hours*, M. iii., 12.
‡ Cp. *Leonard and Gertrude*, iv., ch. 68.

removal of the children from the educative influences of the home and of their father's calling, is one of the chief sources of the ever-increasing family unhappiness in the world. All systems of education which favour this are radically mistaken. They constitute a serious danger of our time."*

Pestalozzi did not regard class divisions as being absolutely fixed, nor did he believe that a child should necessarily pass his life in the circle within which he was born. On the contrary, he recognised that compound of inborn and acquired peculiarities which we call individuality. The schoolmaster in *Leonard and Gertrude* (Part III., Chap. 84) observes the children carefully to find out their special aptitudes, and he would have the way of escape from its surroundings always open to talent. "What an inexpressible pleasure it is to the teacher to find talent —perhaps where least expected, even in the miserable, neglected son of the poorest day-labourer—to come across genius and greatness and to rescue it."†

* *Schweizerblatt*, xxviii., i. ; Seyffarth, vii.
† Seyffarth, viii., 293.

CHAPTER V.

INTELLECTUAL EDUCATION.

Principles of General Application.

PESTALOZZI's division of man's powers into those of "the head, the hand, and the heart," each developing in accordance with its own laws, necessitates the separate treatment of the educational problem according as it is regarded from each one of these points of view. At the same time the unity of the problem as a whole is never lost sight of, and the intimate relations of the intellectual, moral, and physical sides of human nature are repeatedly insisted upon. Before approaching the special problem of intellectual education, it is convenient to point out two general principles of far-reaching practical importance which are for Pestalozzi axiomatic.* They are :

(1) *The impulse to all development lies within.* It is characteristic of organic life that the forces which alone can initiate the changes in form, structure, and function, which we call development, are not communicable. They are given and they are unchangeable. This is the principle of life itself, and the mind is no exception to the general rule. Mental development is as much a process of nature as is the development of the acorn into the oak.

(2) *Development follows exercise.* "The essentially natural and indeed the only means of development our

---

* *V.* Rein, Art. *Pestalozzi.*

82

powers possess is their use." "Morality, love, and faith develop in the practice of right action and in the atmosphere of love and faith, thought-power comes with thinking, and practical skill is acquired by doing."

"Nature impels the eye to see, the ear to hear, the feet to walk, the hand to grasp, the heart to love, and the mind to think."* Rightly managed, "the child thinks as gladly as he walks, and learns as gladly as he eats." The teacher's business is to furnish opportunities for exercise which will foster development in a direction for the determination of which he is responsible. What the child *has* done, he feels he *can* do. He begins to be conscious of power, and to seek opportunity for its exercise. "The feeling of power is for every young child a greater reward and a greater joy than any of those rewards and decorations which men devise for his encouragement in learning. Yet in the schools no use is made of it; we find instead the most pitiable and unnatural substitutes employed. At best they only make the child tolerate that which their teachers wish to cram into them."†

These axioms apply of course throughout, and not merely to intellectual education, with which we are particularly concerned in this chapter.

Definite, Clear and Distinct Ideas.

The object of intellectual education is the acquisition of definite ideas, and the greater part of *How Gertrude Teaches her Children* is devoted to explaining the psychological steps which lead to this ultimate goal, and to an exposition of methods of instruction based upon them. In the tenth letter Pestalozzi tells us what he means by definite

---

* *Christopher and Elizabeth* (Seyffarth), 15, vi., 173.
† *Ibid.*

ideas. *Definiteness* (*Deutlichkeit*) for him means simply *capable of being defined.* " An idea is definite when I can express its essence in words with the greatest possible accuracy and brevity." The result of intellectual training should be definite ideas, " *or rather their statement in words.*"

For all practical purposes I may know the meaning of such words as " horse," " leaf," and yet I may be quite unable to express the ideas in any form of words which would be at the same time " accurate and brief." Probably they take the form of mental pictures which refuse to be expressed within the limits of a definition. They are not therefore *definite*, and from the point of view of Pestalozzi they could not be looked upon as satisfactory results of instruction.

In this insistence upon the definition, Pestalozzi is in agreement with the teaching practice of his day. He rails against the verbalism of the schools, not because the children learn definitions by heart, but because they reach them in the wrong way. The definition was not the coping-stone of a solidly-constructed arch having foundations deep down in the sensory elements of the pupil's mental content ; it was rather the beginning, the middle, and the end of the whole matter. Education was a matter of words all through. At the same time, it was obvious that a view which made the definition the final goal of all teaching processes, even though proper foundations were ensured in the careful accumulation of sensory data, might easily lead to errors in practice. There are many ideas which do not admit of definition at all, and others which, within school age at least, cannot be reduced to fixed formulae without falling into the mistake which Pestalozzi very severely and quite properly criticised. That it led the master himself into error is quite beyond question.

Ideas of objects which are familiar to our senses, as for example those of a horse, a leaf, a house, have of course a place in Pestalozzi's system. They are a necessary preliminary to the definition, and as such they are called *clear* ideas. " The power of *describing* usually precedes that of *definition*. I can describe what is clear to me, but I cannot on that account define it. I only know the object, the individual. *I cannot yet refer it to its genus or its species.*" * The more complete my knowledge of the sensory qualities of an object is, the better I can describe it, that is to say, the clearer is my idea.

Prior to the stage of *clearness* (*Klarheit*) is the stage of *distinctness* (*Bestimmtheit*). This is the actual germ of all our knowledge. It implies simply the separate apprehension of one object, the recognition of a sensation-complex, as standing apart, so to speak, from the relatively unbroken sensory background. To the new-born infant this sensory background is absolutely unbroken ; it is an " undifferentiated sensory continuum," in which sensations of sound, light, contact, etc., are in no way distinguished from each other. The breaking up of this continuum is shown by the child's response to sensory stimuli—other than those which merely excite instinctive activity—as when his eyes follow a moving object, when his crying ceases as the sound of his mother's voice strikes his ear, when he looks about as if to see what he can see. †

The world is still "a swimming sea of confused sense-perceptions," and Pestalozzi, in the true spirit of psychological research, undertook to investigate the processes whereby single perceptions have gradually been separated from other sensations simultaneously presented, whereby

---

* *How Gertrude Teaches her Children*, x., 26.
† *V.* Stout, *Groundwork of Psychology*, p. 14.

the mind has severed that which formerly appeared to be united, and to trace the progress from these vague beginnings to the definite idea.

Although his statement of the problem is admirable, he is not so successful in his method of investigation. He makes the initial mistake of supposing that an adult's proceeding in a conscious effort to disentangle a confused mass of presentations would be a suitable guide to the mental processes of a child unconsciously pursuing the same end. " In a rambling reverie upon my whole purpose, I happened to think of the way a cultivated man must act when he wishes carefully to separate out the details of an object which appears confused and dark before him, and thus gradually to make it clear to himself."[*] In this purely purposive act Pestalozzi distinguishes three steps. The man, he says, will attend to three things : he will try to discover

(a) How many and how many kinds of objects hover before him.

(b) What they look like in respect of form and outline.

(c) What they are called, that is, what sound or word will serve to bring the idea back to his mind.

The word serves to secure the idea, to bring it back into consciousness at any future time, and the qualities of number and form are instinctively sought out because of their universality. *Number, shape,* and *sound* (word) must, therefore, be those starting points of knowledge which he had set out to discover.

The Three " Elementary Means."

As already suggested, Pestalozzi's reasoning from the adult to the child is vitiated by the factor of conscious purpose, which is present in the one case and not in the other.

[*] *How Gertrude Teaches her Children*, vi., 9.

There can be no analogy between the directness of purposeful action and the indirect roundaboutness of action determined by what is called "subjective selection." In this respect, Pestalozzi makes the mistake he himself cautions us against in other places, that of reading into children what is natural to us as adults. He feels the difficulty in respect of the choice of form and number as the elements in which knowledge begins. Why should these sensory data be more fundamental than any other—as, *e.g.*, colour ? His answer is that number and form are common to all objects, a distinction which no other qualities possess. They must therefore be primary, and it is for that reason they "strike us at the first moment and enable us to distinguish one object from another."

He straightway deduces the following didactic principles embodying the *three elementary means*, as he calls these elements :

(a) Children must be taught to regard each object which is presented to them as a unit, *i.e.* as separated from those objects with which it seems to be united.

(b) They must be impressed with the shape of each object, *i.e.* its size and its proportions.

(c) They must be taught the names of all objects known to them at the earliest possible moment.

Pestalozzi regarded these three didactic *principles* as directly parallel to the three *steps* (a), (b), and (c) above, but if we compare (a) in each of the two series, it is clear that there is a confusion between psychical and arithmetical unity. In the principle (a), Pestalozzi has in mind the disintegration of the sensory continuum—the misty sea of sense-perceptions, as he calls it—which takes place when the infant begins to recognise separate sensory complexes as standing forward, so to speak, from the rest.

These sensory complexes are psychical wholes, but they do not involve any idea of number, "which is a rational, not a sense, fact."[*] A child may have the idea of a ball, he may recognise and use the name long before he thinks of *one* ball. When the "cultivated man" resolves the confused presentation into its elements and *counts* them, he is applying powers of abstraction which the young child does not possess, and which the race itself only acquired at a comparatively late period in its history. From a theoretical point of view, therefore, the first of Pestalozzi's "three elementary means" rests upon an unsound basis, and Pestalozzi never arrived at a true explanation of the first steps in mental development, viz., "the movement, disappearance, and reappearance of a sensation complex upon a relatively motionless background."[†]

His view that "form" is the quality in objects which first strikes the child-mind helped to confirm him in the confusion between a psychical and an arithmetical unit. One cannot treat form in teaching without comparison and measurement being involved, and these lead at once to number, or to the idea "more or less," which Pestalozzi, in the eighth letter of *How Gertrude Teaches her Children*, refers to as the basis of numerical relations. The two are inseparable, as the mathematical qualities of objects.

It is obvious that the third elementary means—*sound*— is essentially different from those of *number* and *form* in respect of their relation to an object. Whilst these two are qualities of the object itself, *sound* is an arbitrary sign selected by the race and associated with the object as a convenient sign which serves in speech and in thought to

* Cf. McLellan and Dewey, *Psychology of Number*, ch. 3.
† Wiget, *Pestalozzi and Herbart*.

dispense with the presence of the object. As Pestalozzi says in Letter VI., 10 (c), the word " serves for the representation of objects and for their permanent retention." He is thus careful to distinguish it from the sensory context given by the object itself to the idea. But a paragraph or two later on (VI., 13), number, form, and sound are spoken of as "*qualities of objects*, differing from all other qualities in respect of their universality."

Stripped of these mistakes, the first step in the progress from vague to definite ideas according to Pestalozzi may be represented as follows :

(1) The idea of an object arises from the *isolation* of a sensation mass.

(2) It is at first a vague compound idea, in which *form* is chiefly recognised.

(3) It is held fast by a *word*.

Such a perception is neither *definite* nor *clear*, but in comparison with the chaos from which it arises it is *distinct*, *i.e.*, it is related to an object distinguished from its surroundings. But by changing the psychical into the arithmetical " unity," and by placing the arbitrary vocal sign amongst the perceived qualities of the object itself, Pestalozzi defines a *distinct* idea as one which includes the mathematical qualities of an object (number and form) and its name, without the sensory qualities—colour, smell, taste, etc. It is already an abstraction and the first link in the chain which leads to definitions.

At the end of Letter VI., pp. 13-15, Pestalozzi abruptly changes these three elements which constitute *distinctness* in ideas—" the three elementary means "—into spheres of knowledge, in *each* of which the whole development from vague intuitions to definite ideas has to be gone through. The *three elementary means* become the three elementary subjects—arithmetic, writing (drawing), and reading. The fact that he had tried at Stanz to solve the problem of teaching these subjects by resolving them into their elements probably explains why, in the psychological analysis already described, he fixed his attention on number, form, and sound rather than on the qualities of things which first appeal to the child.

Pestalozzi's Analysis of Mental Progress.

We are now in a position to examine Pestalozzi's whole analysis of mental development from vague to definite ideas in reference to the " whole art of methodical teaching." In Letter VI., 5, there are three consecutive rules, each with three clauses. The object of instruction, he says, is attained in three steps :

I. (a) *Separating* the objects, thereby removing the confusion in the sense-impressions.

(b) Bringing together again in representations the objects which are alike, thereby making them *clear.*

(c) Raising these perfectly clear ideas to definite conceptions.

and he adds that these steps are attained by—

II. (a) Presenting the confused sense-conceptions *separately.*

(b) Changing the conditions under which the observations are separately made.

(c) Bringing them finally into connection with the remaining content of our knowledge.

Thus, he says, our knowledge grows

III. (a) From vagueness to *distinctness* (*Bestimmtheit*).

(b) From distinctness to *clearness* (*Klarheit*).

(c) From clearness to *definiteness* (*Deutlichkeit*).

We may, with Wiget, adduce the parallel of Letter VI., 13,—

IV. (a) Through the consciousness of the unity, form, and name of an object we attain to *distinct* knowledge.

(b) Through the gradual extension of our knowledge to all its remaining qualities it becomes *clear*.

(c) Through the knowledge of the connection of its distinguishing characteristics it becomes *definite*.

and of VI., 15.   Progress in all three elementary subjects (reading, writing, and arithmetic) advances from

V. (a) Vague to distinct observation.

(b) Distinct observation to clear representation.

(c) Clear representation to definite conception.

By bringing Pestalozzi's various statements into line in this way, it is possible to determine exactly what he means. Although worded differently, the final clause (c) in each case is intended to present the same fact viewed either as process or result.   The definition, it will be remembered, is the crowning point of instruction, and the definition is the statement of the relation of the thing defined to the whole content of our knowledge.   It gathers up the distinguishing features of a class of objects and expresses them as belonging to a system.   This is the stage to which (c) in each of these parallel statements refers.   The first clauses (a) are similarly in harmony and obviously all refer to that step in the forward movement which he has called *distinctness*.

Abstraction.

Comparing now the clauses marked (b) there are some important differences.   By analogy we should expect them all to refer to the step which Pestalozzi calls *clearness*, that stage in our knowledge of a thing which enables us to describe it, and this is clearly meant in iv. b, but how we are to pass from iv. b to iv. c is not manifest until we look at i. *b* and ii. *b*, where a stage beyond that of mere " clearness " is hinted at, or rather a process is suggested which to some extent presupposes "clearness." Although the word "clear" occurs in i. *b*, the process of comparison invited by calling to mind similar objects, and the process of changing the conditions under which the objects are separately observed (ii. *b*), obviously point to a process of abstraction by means of which the casual qualities may be separated from the essential—a process which comes to a head in (*c*), *i.e.* in definition.

It is interesting to compare the results of this analysis with Pestalozzi's statements in Letter V. The point of view is reversed. He begins, "Everything which touches my senses is for me only so far a means of arriving at a correct judgment as its appearance makes me sensible of its unchanging and unchangeable essence" (v. 2, *a*); we attain to this " by putting together objects which are alike in essence, thereby weakening the one-sided, preponderating impression made by the striking qualities of single objects (v. 2, *d*), but as a preliminary step it is necessary to be clear about the qualities of single objects, employing as many senses as possible to that end (v. 2, *c*, *f*). This amounts to saying that we reach *definite* ideas by means of abstraction, the materials for which are furnished by *clear* ideas of single objects. Going over similar ground in the *Swansong* (70), he explicitly refers to abstraction as the means whereby man passes from the stage of sense-perception to the stage of thought proper.

That he understood the nature of this process and its place in the course of development is shown by his remarks in the preface to the *Observation Lessons in Number-relations*, Part II. " When the mother lays peas, leaves, pebbles, sticks, and whatever else it may be, upon the table for the child to count, she must not say,—that is *one*, but

that is *one stick*, that is *one stone*; and again when she
points to two, she must not say, that is twice one, but that
is twice one stone, or that is two stones, two leaves. . . . If
the mother shows the child different kinds of objects,
such as peas, stones, etc., and teaches him to recognise
and name them as one pea, two peas, three peas, etc.,
repeated in this manner the words one, two, three remain
always unchanged, whilst the words peas, pebbles, etc.,
change according to the object shown; this combination
of stability and change gives rise to the abstract notion of
number in the mind of the child, that is to say the definite
consciousness of more or less, independently of the objects
themselves. Yet the consciousness of the real relations
is never lost." This " inextinguishable consciousness of
reality" gives life to the definition, and so preserves it
from the reproach of mere verbalism which marked the
education current in Pestalozzi's day.

Bringing together the various steps in the process of
advance from " the misty sea of sense-perceptions to
definite ideas," we get—

(1) The apprehension and naming of separate objects.
(2) The apprehension of the qualities of those objects in
    detail.
(3) The comparison of objects alike in essence, but dis-
    similar in certain features or in the conditions of
    their presentation.
(4) The abstraction of the essential qualities, *i.e.* the
    permanent from the casual and changing.
(5) The definition.

These are all expressed or implied in Pestalozzi's
analysis. ' It will be noted that throughout he is dealing
only with sensory presentations, the whole content of which
is given by the sensory activities (1) and (2) above.
Comparison can add nothing to this content. Hence the

fundamental importance of observation for all knowledge.
" The final ripening of each and every general notion is
essentially dependent on the perfected force of its first in-
ception.   Everything that is imperfect in the germ will be
crippled in its growth."*

Observation (*Anschauung*).

" Life educates," says Pestalozzi in the *Swansong* (70),
actual contact with sensory circumstance gives impulse
and nourishment to development.   Ideas are *definite* when
experience has exhausted its powers of adding to their
clearness, *i.e.*, when further observation can bring to light
no additional qualities, when the work of our sensory
activities has been completed, and the necessary abstraction has been thought out.

This principle, viz., that *actual sensory experience, carefully organised and systematically worked out* is the only
sound basis of instruction, was not only the first to come
out in the historical development of Pestalozzi's pedagogy,
it was also, for him, the most important of all his contributions to educational science, the centre of his whole
system.   His earliest teaching practice was, of course, connected with his little son Jaqueli.   His diary reveals his
method.   Paternally directed observation leads the child
to see that water flows down hill, that some things
float and others sink in water.   In trying to teach him the
conception of number, he discovered *how a knowledge of
words, which are mere sounds to a child, may become a real
obstacle to his obtaining a knowledge of truth.*†
Throughout his career he held fast to this principle.   In
the *Schweizerblatt* we read " that the man who in his youth

* Letter X., 27, 28.
† *V.* De Guimps, *Life of Pestalozzi*, cl iv.

has not caught butterflies, nor wandered over hill and dale
hunting for plants, etc., in spite of all desk work, will not
get far in his subject. He will always be exposed to
blunders which otherwise he would never have made." In
rainy weather toadstools grow fast on every dung-heap;
and in the same way definitions, not founded on sense impression, produce, just as quickly, a fungus-like wisdom,
which dies rapidly in the sunlight.* In his last pedagogic
utterances he returned to the subject, treating it with un-
usual fulness in the *Swansong*.† "The child must
learn to know a *few* things, *e.g.*, of animals, some of the
mammals, the birds, the fishes, which are in his immediate
neighbourhood, but these few thoroughly; he should be
led to observe with elementary exactness the various forms
of water and its transitions from one form to the other in
nature (dew, rain, vapour, frost, hail, snow, ice), and the
influence it exerts in these various forms upon other
natural objects; in the kitchen he should see the dissolving of sugar and salt and their recovery by evapora-
tion."‡

Brought up on lines such as these, a boy will be ready
in the future for the scientific pursuit of any branch of
knowledge. His work will be sound because it will be
guided by the habit of facing hard fact acquired in the
earliest stages of his education. The school journey was a
regular institution at Yverdun, as we gather from
Pestalozzi's legitimate boast in the Lenzburg Address,§
that although from 120 to 130 boys in different
divisions had made journeys on foot lasting two or three
weeks, and including the ascent of formidable mountains,

* *How Gertrude Teaches her Children*, x.
† M. iv., 256.
‡ *V.* also *Leonard and Gertrude*, as summarised in pp. 29 ff.
§ M. iii., 498.

except for a cold or two, they had all come back none the
worse for their exposure to the very changeable weather.
Contemporary independent accounts of the method of
teaching geography,* the walks, the measuring and judging
of distance, and actual observations in the neighbourhood
of Yverdun, and the exercises thereon—all show how
Pestalozzi emphasised concrete experience in intellectual
education. He particularly combats the substitution of
pictures for objects. In most cases, they either put before
the child what he cannot see in Nature, or they are pictures
of things which he might see every day. "Comenius and
Basedow substituted a painted world for the real one."

Concrete Mental Development: Language.

We have now arrived at a knowledge of Pestalozzi's
analysis of the process of intellectual development, noting
particularly the emphasis he places upon the first steps to
clearness, and the manner in which the advance from
knowledge of the particular to knowledge of the general
(from *clearness* to *definiteness*) is made.

We may now enquire when this definiteness begins, and
when the steps in mental progress take place. Pestalozzi
hopes to put it in the power of every mother to give her
child instruction in the elements of knowledge, and in his
treatment of sound as the basis of language teaching he
goes back to the cradle period of the child's life. Clearly
he is not thinking merely of the school, or of what we are
accustomed to regard as a child's "learning time." "Life
educates," and education begins with the first breath.

Pestalozzi has worked out the notion of concrete
development most fully in relation to language. It was

---

* *Vide* Appendix II., p. 208.

the work he took most pride in, and the principles underlying it are, therefore, important elements in his educational theory.   In the tenth letter of *How Gertrude Teaches
her Children* he gives the grounds for the linguistic methods
described in the seventh.   Broadly speaking, he aims at
enabling the child " to acquire speech in exactly the same
gradual way in which Nature has given it to the human
race."   The " course of nature " in this case means the
historical progress of mankind as a whole, not the psychological progress which each individual necessarily (*i.e.*
because of his nature) follows, and which the phrase
" according to nature " usually means for Pestalozzi.   To
assist him in determining the chief steps in the development of speech, and in accordance with them to fix the
order of speech instruction, he looked for guidance to the
course which racial development had actually taken in the
matter of language.

He there distinguishes three epochs :

I. The period of mimicry, the mere making of sounds
   in imitation of animals or inanimate nature.

II. The period of special names for special objects—of
    hieroglyphics and separate words for objects and
    activities.

III. The period in which conspicuous differences
     were observed and named, developing much
     later into the power of making one word mean
     much.

Racially, the process has taken thousands of years, yet
the child must learn the art in a few months.   Obviously
he must take the shortest road to the desired end.   It
must be exactly the same course as Nature has followed,
but without following such a circuitous route as blind
Nature has taken.   For Pestalozzi's purpose the broad
epochs provide the necessary guidance

The steps in the teaching of speech as given in Letter VII. are:

I. The learning of *sounds*. It includes the training of the organs of speech, and the regular practice of all the sounds in the language. Instead of crooning at haphazard over her infant's cradle, the mother is to repeat these phonetic elements in a systematic way. " The whole compass of them is to reach the child's consciousness before he is able to speak." As this power develops he will repeat these sounds in imitation of his mother, instead of the unanalysable prattle which is " blind Nature's " way. Exercises in single tones and sequences of tones in speech and song are provided in the *Hints on Teaching, Spelling, and Reading*, published in 1801.

II. The learning of *words*. It is in the main concerned with the teaching of names of objects. To facilitate this he projected a *Mother's Book*.* Lists of names of all the most important objects in nature, history, geography, human callings and relations are given in exercises in reading. Children easily learn these lists by heart, and later instruction is made much easier, for in this chaotic collection are materials for the house that is to be built.

III. The learning of *language*, which includes the means of expressing all that the child recognises in an object. It divides into—

(a) Expressing himself about number and form.

(b) Expressing himself about the other qualities of objects, derived as they may be from further sensory acquaintance, or from the exercises of abstraction, imagination, and judgment in respect of them.

* This book never existed. It is not *The Mother's Book*, which has already been described. *V.* also App. III.

(*c*) Expressing himself about the connections of objects with each other in their varying conditions of time, number, and proportion.

The relation of these three steps in the process of language teaching to the steps which Pestalozzi lays down as those through which the race has passed in the acquisition of speech are obvious. We may also note in both cases the correspondence to the order of development of ideas. The period of mimicry, and of the practising of sounds is that of *vague* ideas ; the period of word making and word learning (*i.e.* the apprehension of single objects and naming them) is that of *distinct* ideas; whilst in the period of language proper, we have first of all *clear* ideas leading finally up to *definite* ones. It is to be noted that number and form fall into the third (language) period. Knowledge and linguistic power develop together, and the periods of development in the child correspond to the periods of development in the race. In the Lenzburg Address Pestalozzi distinctly speaks of two such periods: (1) the period of observation (*Anschauungsepoche*), and (2) the period of the general notion (*Begriffsepoche*). During the period of observation the child is chiefly occupied in acquiring distinct and clear ideas. Distinctness and clearness are both the result of observation, indeed the latter properly includes the former, and the efficiency of the work done at this time, determines the character of that accomplished in the period of greater maturity.

When Steps in Development take place.

But Pestalozzi drew no hard and fast line of temporal demarcation between these periods. Before he comes to school, the mother is to lead the child to abstract notions of number, and in various other ways he is led to work out the ordered sensory presentations whilst he is still at home.

Exercise in careful observation over a wide field stimulates the latent power to generalise and deduce conclusions.

The child is intellectually ready for school when this capacity has been in this way awakened,* but the observing powers do not cease to grow at this point. In fact, as knowledge grows the powers of observation increase. " One who is in the habit of examining the structure of plants, and is conversant with a system of botany, will discover a number of distinguishing characteristics of a flower, for instance, which remain wholly unnoticed by one who knows nothing of that science."†

There is of course a period in the life of every child which is inaccessible to definite ideas of every kind. Observation is logically and psychologically prior to abstraction and definition, but the power to compare and generalise appears very early, and in Pestalozzi's view is best assisted by lessons in number and form. " Elementary education recognises in number and form the simplest natural means of forwarding the transition from the already formed power of observation to the more perfect power of judgment, and of establishing finally the foundation of the higher power of abstraction." " In counting and measuring we have the first exercise in this direction."‡ The reason is of course that these elements are constantly being presented to the child in the shape of the world of objects amidst which he lives.

The general notion, the definite idea, is absolutely conditioned by the range of observation. If the necessary material is not forthcoming in experience, *the general notion must not be formulated.* "The child's circle of

---

* Lenzburg Address, M. vol. iii., p. 537.
† *Letters to Greaves*, p. 101.
‡ *Swansong*, pars. 26, 70, 98 (M. vol. iv.).

experience determines, therefore, not only the *starting point* but also the *horizon* of his thought.* If we regard the range of observation and conception as two concentric circles, then the first may include the second, but this second must never go beyond the first. The maxim, 'Life educates,' which fastens the observation of the child to his own individual situation, keeps his thoughts within the same limits."† Any attempt to force its exercise beyond these limits, as by hurrying on the learning of logical rules, or by premature judgment in relation to objects only superficially observed, will have the same effect as forcing precocity in any other direction. The powers of thought will " swell up, grow vague, weaken, and finally stand still." Solid progress in thought power can only come in one way—by practice in careful and correct combination, separation, and comparison of objects actually observed.

Pestalozzi's Formalism.

As Pestalozzi so frequently insists upon the education of the "powers of the mind," the question has not unnaturally been raised as to whether he might properly be called a formalist or a realist in his educational doctrine. Did he hold that thought power exercised and developed in in any particular direction would be available in any sphere? The doctrine of independent powers certainly suggests this, and his view of the formal value of arithmetic as training in the power of abstraction, as well as much of his practice and the practice of his imitators gave good ground for the contemporary criticism which concentrated itself upon this point.

* *Swansong*, M. iv., 219. † Wiget, *op. cit.*

Yet Pestalozzi was too keen an observer to hold such an opinion, and every day's experience showed him that a man with excellent judgment in one direction may be of little use in another. He always insists that the exercise of judgment which education provides, should have direct reference to the sphere of life from which the pupil comes and in which he is likely to remain. "A thousand examples show us how innumerable men, even scientifically educated, have not been trained to think seriously and habitually in regard to the actual circumstances of their daily life, so that in every situation which lies outside their profession, their judgments and opinions are hopelessly untrustworthy." As with thought, so with observation, our powers do not develop generally, but only within a certain sphere of habitual operations, within the limits of the "circle of thought." * It is life that educates.

But certain absurdities in Pestalozzi's practice, which are to be explained by his psychology, gave strong support to the charge of formalism so far as his "elementary method" was concerned, a charge which the Lenzburg Address is at pains to refute. "I let children of three years old spell the wildest nonsense merely because it was nonsensically hard."† "I was not so much concerned that my children should learn to spell, to read, and to write as I was anxious that their mental powers should develop through these exercises in as all-round and effective a way as possible. to that end I made them spell words by heart before they knew the alphabet, and the whole room could spell the hardest words before they knew a single letter." ‡ These are examples of the "training of the powers" view, which, together with the verbalism of much of Pestalozzi's teach

* Cp. *Swansong*, M. iv., pp. 248-50.
† *How Gertrude Teaches her Children*, i., 42.
‡ *V*. Stanz Letter, p. 195.

ing, are the stock examples of the contradiction between
Pestalozzi's theory and practice. As a matter of fact, the
practice is the outcome of a principle (viz. that power
comes with exercise) wrongly applied, bringing it thereby
into strong opposition with the principle that exercise
must have meaning for the child, that is to say, must
have life.

Pestalozzi's verbalism was further accentuated by his
view of the function of words. We have seen how in the
step prior to the teaching of language, the child is to learn
long lists of names of objects with which he is not yet
acquainted. By this means "the representation of the
object is preceded by the fluency of the sound which describes the object, and from the moment when by observation the child can combine the object with the sound
which denotes it, he cannot possibly forget it." Pestalozzi
is here thinking of the nursery where the young child
acquires many words whose content is at first exceedingly
thin, but additional experience deepens their meaning and
narrows their application. This natural method of
acquiring a vocabulary in early childhood is extended by
Pestalozzi to the school. Amongst the points that Krusi
notes in the method at Burgdorf is "that through a well-
arranged nomenclature indelibly impressed, a general foundation for all kinds of knowledge was laid."* In this way the
child was to enjoy the advantages of one whose home is in
a great house of business, and who therefore acquires every
day from his cradle upwards the names of countless
objects.* The words are thus "ready like nets to catch
meanings, as experience gives the opportunity."†

This practice of Pestalozzi's struck Herbart very forcibly,

* *How Gertrude Teaches her Children*, i., 43.
† Wiget, *op. cit.*

as he tells us in his review of *How Gertrude Teaches her Children*.* He admitted that the little children seemed to enjoy the exercise, and in talking over the matter with Pestalozzi it occurred to him that possibly an *inner sense of the meaning* of what is being taught to them is even more important than its instantaneous apprehension. "Most of that which they learned by heart had to do with objects immediately about them. The child left the school with his words in his head, saw the object, and now for the first time perhaps realised what the words meant, and that in a much more perfect way than he would have done, had the teacher tried to explain them through other words.

"The lesson gives the word and puts together what should go together in thought, time and opportunity attach ideas to the words, and fuse into an intimate whole what were until then, only laid side by side. At the same time we must not forget that Pestalozzi was dealing with little children. To them a word is not as it is to us, merely the sign of a thing, but a thing in itself. They stop over the sound, and only when that is quite familiar to them, do they learn to forget it in the thing."

If further support were wanted for what developed into an empty teaching of words, Pestalozzi's view of the nature and function of language provided it. The point is, as usual, excellently put by Wiget: "Since language is originally 'the giving back of all the impressions which nature in her whole course has made upon the race,' and since, according to Herder—Pestalozzi's authority for the origin of language—' the impression of a thing must be similar upon all the members of one species,' so Pestalozzi (perhaps under the influence of older traditions which ascribed a certain reality to words), held it for possible,

---

* Herbart's *Sämmtliche Werke*, Band I., S. 142.

' by means of her spoken sounds, to awaken in the child the very impressions which these tones have always produced on the race.'* And this idea took such hold of him that the principle of observation was overshadowed. Things were pushed aside by words, and into the place of nature teaching the dictionary stepped.† The contradiction between theory and practice is thus again 'a contradiction between two principles, justified in themselves, but with regard to the range of their applicability not sufficiently delimited.' "

The "Elementary Method."

Pestalozzi frequently compares the development of the mind to that of a plant or a tree. In *How Gertrude Teaches her Children* (iv. 10), we are asked to consider how Nature produces the largest tree from a tiny seed; " first she produces a scarcely perceptible shoot, then just as imperceptibly, daily and hourly, by gradual stages, she unfolds first the beginnings of the stem, then the bough, then the branch, then the extreme twig on which hangs the perishable leaf." As a picture of the growth of a tree, there is a good deal wanting in this sketch, but the " gradual imperceptible advance " struck him forcibly as " Nature's way," and as he " *knew* that the mechanism of human nature is essentially subject to the same laws as those by which physical nature unfolds her powers," he arrived at a most important practical principle which is the essence of his " Elementary Method." " Try to make, in every act, graduated steps of knowledge, in which each new idea is only a small, scarcely perceptible addition to that which is already known."

* *How Gertrude Teaches her Children*, vii., 46.
† *Ibid.*, vii., 34.

The point, of course, is that instruction is to be adapted to the powers of the pupil. " Everything which the child has to learn must be proportioned to his strength, getting more complicated and difficult in the same degree as his powers of attention, of judgment, and thought increase."* But the psychology of attention teaches us the inappropriateness of the " scarcely perceptible additions" which are to govern the teacher's gradua-tion of his subject-matter. Again, Pestalozzi fails to see just how far his principles—especially those derived from analogy with the life of the organic world—apply, and the development of the doctrine of " scarcely per-ceptible additions" into that of " uninterrupted con-tinuity" produced the absurdities in *The Mother's Book*,† which drew upon him the scorn of many critics. " Ele-mentary " for Pestalozzi, in the Lenzburg Address, for example, means " without gaps," " unbroken continuity," and as the *Report to Parents* informs us, the great problem of the Institute was to accomplish a gradua-tion of all the subjects of instruction in accordance with with the demands of this principle.

Psychical progress is unbroken, and its daily advance, like that of the plant, is imperceptible, and the course of education must be similarly unbroken, accompanying step by step, the increase of power with suitably graduated stimuli. A course of education organised on these lines and embracing the intellectual, physical (practical), and moral sides of human nature, Pestalozzi calls " Elemen-tary," and the whole method he calls the " Elementary Method." Its nature is discussed in the Lenzburg Address,‡ though it is not always easy to distinguish the vague

---

* *Report to Parents* (1807), Morf, p. 48.
† *V.* Appendix III., p. 213.   ‡ *V.* Appendix III., p. 218.

generalities of Niederer from the more directly practical views of Pestalozzi.

The search for the " elements " which lie at the base of such an " elementary " scheme of instruction led Pestalozzi to a point of view which has received a good deal of attention in recent years. In the *Report to Parents* we read : " The Institute recognises only one course of instruction for each subject, viz. that which, in perfect harmony with the course of development of human nature, follows the nature and the development of the subject itself." " We put our children on the road which the discoverer of the subject himself took, and had to take. We put into his hand the thread of its extension, and the steps of its development, as they have been pursued by the race, in order that he may himself independently seize and put to use in the same direction the materials to hand, going as far as his powers will allow." Although this report bears the mark of Niederer's editorship, the same idea is involved in Pestalozzi's treatment of language in *How Gertrude Teaches her Children.*

The ideal was, of course, impossible in practice; men of science had not at that time worked at the history of their respective subjects ; but the suggestion is interesting, and although it can hardly be applied in detail to all subjects, the practice of teaching science historically is not now-a-days uncommon, and distinguished authorities have recommended its more frequent adoption.*

Law of Physical Distance.

We have seen, on the one hand, the steps through which the mind advances from vague to definite ideas, in which

* Cp. *The Heuristic Method of Teaching* (Armstrong), in which the idea of putting children at the point of view of the investigator is worked out.

the latent power of abstraction plays the final part, and, on the other hand, the nature of the graduation which the subject-matter of instruction must undergo in order to come into line with the progress of mental power. The problem of bringing these two—the growing mind and the objects which contribute to its nourishment—into effective relation is yet to be faced. Pestalozzi found its solution in the *Law of Physical Distance*, which he enunciates in the sixth letter of *How Gertrude Teaches her Children*.

Here we read "that clearness of knowledge varies according to the nearness and remoteness of the objects which are in touch with my senses." All that surrounds us reaches our senses in impressions which are confused, and difficult to make clear and definite, in proportion to its distance from us, and on the contrary everything is distinct and easy to make clear and definite in proportion as it lies near to our five senses. "As a physical being you are nothing but your five senses; consequently the clearness or mistiness of your ideas must absolutely rest upon the nearness or remoteness with which all external objects touch these five senses, that is, yourself." And as the nearest object for the exercise of the senses is one's self, one's knowledge of one's self must be the starting point of one's knowledge of truth.

This law, literally understood and applied in the "elementary" sense, produced the first six exercises of *The Mother's Book*. The statement is not a happy one, and although Pestalozzi had glimpses of the real truth, he was unable to see the absurdities perpetrated by Krusi's contribution to the book from which he hoped so much. At the end of Letter V. we read: "man can only learn the truth of the world in its physical aspects in that measure in which the objects which actually come within his observation are thoroughly familiar." It is clear from this that Pestalozzi does not mean by his "law of physical distance" that we really cannot know anything which has not reached us through observation, but rather that what has so reached us is the means by which our knowledge actually may transcend our experience. That which actual experience teaches is *psychically* nearest, it is liveliest, the most intimate portion of our mental content, and by its means we are able to apprehend that which is physically remote.*

This is what Pestalozzi tells us in Letter VII. "Lastly," he says, "knowledge derived through our senses has an analogical value ; by its means I learn the characteristics of things which have never come within the range of my observation. My knowledge is thus greatly advanced; it is no longer dependent entirely upon my senses, but the whole range of my mind's powers may work up the materials my senses provide." Whilst the "physical distance law" is approximately true of very early life, so soon as a stock of well-established sensory knowledge is acquired, analogical observation sets the child free to the extent that he may learn of things far removed from his own experience—of things which never even happened or existed at all—provided that he is in possession of images which will serve to build up the new picture. His existing knowledge only fixes limits to what we may teach him, because it furnishes the materials for its proper apprehension.

The most striking effect of Pestalozzi's *Law of Physical Nearness*, as enunciated in the sixth letter, was that it led him, in the *Swansong*, to reject history as a subject for

---

* Students will compare with this the doctrine of apperception as enunciated by the Herbartians—a truer statement of what Pestalozzi *felt*, but could not express.

study in schools. "It is utter nonsense that men who have no living acquaintance with the world as it stands before their eyes, should wish to be made acquainted with the spirit of a bygone world, removed from the world of to-day by hundreds and even thousands of years. In this subject, one can do no more than to exercise the children in mnemonically memorising extended lists of names of men and places which history proper demands."

It is the same principle more reasonably applied which made him regard "modern languages" as prior to dead languages. The subject-matter of the books read in modern languages is obviously more nearly related to the child's stock of ideas than that of the classical authors. "Homer, Plato, and Tacitus are not reading for younger children, their contents being beyond their power of comprehension."* The odd conjunction of names shows how completely the "law of distance" had taken hold of Pestalozzi.

Niederer appreciated the law much more clearly in the psychical sense than his master. He holds it as the principle which decides whether or not a subject is suitable for a child at a particular moment. In the *Report to Parents*, already quoted, we read: "Each child shall be taught that which he has to learn at the time his nature calls for it, for this is the proof that his sensibility and power are ready for it." Unlike Pestalozzi, he approved of history teaching on condition that it was brought into harmony with the development of the pupil, and he regarded Herbart's example in reading Homer with his pupil as a sound pedagogic introduction to the subject. Niederer's influence probably also accounts for the fact that history always occupied a place in the curriculum at Yverdun.

* Lenzburg Address, M. iii., 512.

Individuality in Intellectual Education.

One may note, in concluding this chapter, a striking passage in the *Report to Parents*, which is sufficient to demonstrate the fact that in spirit at least Pestalozzi was the reverse either of a formalist or of a mechanical educator. We have already seen that in respect of the graduation of the subject-matter of instruction two principles governed the teacher's action, (1) the historical principle, *i.e.* the actual history of the subject as such; and (2) the principle of uninterrupted continuity of advance in scarcely perceptible steps. So far the children do not come specifically into account, except in so far as these principles correspond respectively to a suspected parallelism between mental development in the child and the race, and to a parallelism between the growth of a plant and the growth of the mind.

In practice, however, Pestalozzi found that children differed in the rapidity with which they followed the path the teacher had laid down for them, and that the same child advanced in one direction more quickly than in another. The school was therefore organised so that the same subject was taught throughout the various classes at the same time, to make it possible to transfer the children from class to class in accordance with their actual progress.

But this principle of suiting the instruction to the child was carried further. What each child was to learn and when he was to begin, was determined by his particular nature. The subjects which appeal to him are thereby proved to be those particularly suited to his powers. If the psychological moment has been found, he will learn in a month what otherwise might take years. Further, continues the report, " we try to discover on which side a child is strongest, in order to make that the centre, so to speak, of his intellectual activity, or that we may use this special interest as a thread by means of which we may lead him towards a life of intellectual independence, having confidence in his own efforts and never ceasing to widen the circle of his activity. And whilst as a matter of fact there is no child who is universal in his capacity, so is there none who does not possess special talent in some one direction, and who, given the opportunity, would not excel therein. What is more, the time when a particular aptitude may develop is quite uncertain. A boy suddenly shows a new feeling for a subject which previously had not the smallest influence upon him.... Clearly then, as it seems to me, the nature of the child must determine all the details of his education, and an educational institution must be so organised as to afford room for adaptation to the inclination and needs of the individual pupil."

CHAPTER VI.

PRACTICAL EDUCATION.

Intellectual and Physical Foundations.

" To have knowledge without practical power, to have insight and yet to be incapable of applying it in everyday life—could an unfriendly spirit devise a more fearful lot for a human being than this ? " The feeling of practical power and its exercise are as essential to man as knowledge and thought, and indeed knowing and doing, impression and expression, are so closely connected that when one ceases, the other ceases with it. It is therefore as important to cultivate practical capacity—without which our wants and wishes cannot be satisfied—and to carry it through to the same degree of perfection, as it is to train thought-power and intellectual insight. Both alike are fundamental necessities of the human organism.*

In this chapter we are concerned with the cultivation of practical capacity (*Kunstkraft*), with the " psychological unfolding of the many-sided physical powers which dwell in the child's nature."

The letters which constitute *How Gertrude Teaches her Children* only treat this part of the problem of education very slightly. Pestalozzi's more detailed ideas upon the subject must be looked for in other of his writings. Thus it is in the *Swansong* † that he tells us what he means by

* *How Gertrude Teaches her Children*, xii., 5.
† Mann, iv., pp. 190-1.

" practical capacity." The term includes the power of giv-ing external expression to the products of the intellect, of giving external effectiveness to the impulses of the heart, and of performing the practical duties which belong to home and business life. Without dwelling upon the obvious defects of this statement as a logical classification, it is useful as showing us how widely the term is to be under-stood; it implies effectiveness in action of any and every kind.

The impulse to action lies, of course, in human nature itself. The teacher's business is to understand the con-ditions, psychological and physiological, under which action may be effectively controlled and purposefully directed. In attacking this problem, Pestalozzi, as always, endeavours to go to the root of the matter. He finds that the foundations of practical power are partly intellectual and partly physical. Definite action implies an idea of what is to be done, as well as the power of doing it. The importance of this preliminary intellectual condition, as we may call it, is well brought out in Pestalozzi's treat-ment of drawing—the typical school dexterity—to which he has paid a good deal of attention in the seventh of the Gessner Letters. As we shall see, the necessary initial ideas are partly intellectual and purposive and partly ideas of movement.

Before drawing of any kind is attempted, he tells us, the child should be able to apprehend form. A child cannot draw an object properly "until he has ideas about the proportion of the form, and is able to express himself concerning them." To this end he devised what he called an "A B C of observation." "This alphabet of observa-tion," says Dean Ith in his report,* "is a square, decimally divided by horizontal, perpendicular, and slanting lines,"

* *V.* p. 52.

which was to be applied to the analysis of forms as the alphabet is used for the analysis of sounds. It was at first used in actual measurement, the divided square being traced on transparent horn which could be superposed upon other forms. In the course of this exercise, a feeling for proportion insensibly arises, by means of which "measurements" may be made without mechanical aid.

The "power to observe form" has now been acquired. Obviously only the geometrical aspects of objects represented or seen "in the flat" is referred to. So far, however, "the eye has been trained," not in the sense of having been made optically more delicate, but in the only way which "sense training" can have a meaning. It is the *mind* that has been trained by exercise to deal effectively with certain sense material. The "idea of measurement" has been acquired, which of course involves ideas of proportion and the power to express proportion numerically—as twice this or that, the half of something else, etc. Thus "the idea of drawing is not only founded upon the power of the hand, but upon the inward processes of the human mind." So far there has been no thought of manual dexterity, but the preliminary geometrical and arithmetical ideas have been in process of formation.

What is true of drawing is true of all dexterities. It is essential for the efficiency of practical power of any kind, artistic or technical, that the "powers of thought and judgment should undergo a preliminary training, which always begins with the exercise of the observing powers "*—not, of course, generally, but in the particular direction demanded by the sphere of practical activity with which we are concerned.

Having secured the necessary intellectual foundations, the physical side of the training begins. The aim now is

* *Swansong*, M. iv., 191.

to establish practical skill (*Fertigkeit*), which rests on the highest possible degree of what Pestalozzi calls "nerve-tact," that is to say, upon the ready and certain action of delicate nerve coordinations which ensure certainty of movement in the hundred different directions demanded by a complicated physical action. Here again, however, is a parallel mental condition. Muscular control from the side of mind, rests ultimately upon "sensations of motion" which are only obtained by moving; hence, Pestalozzi points out that while in order "to know" we may often remain passive, in order to acquire practical skill and power we must *do*. Sensations of motion frequently repeated and attended to acquire a certain fixity as "motor ideas," and as such are instantly at the service of conceived action involving them. The perfect coordination of these "motor ideas" is the mental parallel to the nerve-tact of which Pestalozzi speaks.

These then are the preliminary physical (physiological) and mental conditions of practical power. Advance in physical dexterity is, however, in no way parallel to the intellectual advance described in the last chapter. The latter depends upon the purely mental power of abstraction, the former upon mere repetition. Pestalozzi puts it in this way: "The laws which govern the development of the physical powers are physical, because the mechanism which gives power to the human limbs is itself physical."*

" Mind " must always enter into Training.

At the same time, in endeavouring to provide practice, the intellectual background is not to be overlooked. Mind is always behind effective action, and merely mechanical exercise of the limbs is deficient as an educational instru-

* *Swansong*, M. iv., 236. Cp. also James, *Text-Book of Psychology*, chap. x.

ment, because it makes no demands upon intellectual activity. *The practiçe of purely mechanical exercises which are not the result of an intellectual stimulus has no part in human education;* such exercises tend to blunt intellectual and moral power.*

This is a vital principle of Pestalozzianism. It means simply that the child is to associate himself with the action, that what he is doing must correspond to a purpose or to a need of his own. The idea is well put again in regard to early lessons in drawing: " Let the child use his chalk or pencil freely, assisted and occasionally stimulated by his teacher, but do not force him into directions which do not appeal to him. He will finally become sensible of the need for greater accuracy. At that moment methodical training may properly begin." " Not until the thought arises in the child that his mother might help him in what he wishes to do, but cannot do properly, has the time come for the guidance of the teacher's art to find ready access to the child's mind."† The teacher is to guard against being regarded as an interfering person, and also to avoid the danger of crushing the child's spontaneity by drilling him into a machine.

In the face of the infinite complexities of movement involved in the many specialised forms of practical skill, and in face of Pestalozzi's constant endeavour to elementarise all forms of instruction, it is not surprising to find him considering the possibility of discovering an " A B C of practical power" which "should be a series of exercises advancing gradually from the simplest to the most complicated dexterities." This third "alphabet" should include the elements of all physical activity; it should be a "general gymnastic of power." "Unhappily," he says,

* Lenzburg Address, M. iii., 470.
† *Swansong*, M. iv., 237.

"this A B C of practical power is not yet found, and one rarely hears of anybody trying to work it out. Earnestly worked at the problem should present no great difficulty." "The alphabet must start from the simplest natural expressions of physical power in which lie the foundations of the most complex human dexterities: striking and carrying, thrusting and throwing, pulling and twisting, wrestling and swinging."*

Although he has not himself worked out such a system as he suggests, his occasional references suggest important principles. It is clear that in Pestalozzi's view, general physical training is to precede such specialised physical training as would be given by learning one particular dexterity—as for example that involved in a skilled manual occupation.

A one-sided training like this would be bad for two reasons. On the purely physical side it fixes certain movements prematurely, and makes it difficult either to acquire skill in a new direction or to rearrange, even in a slight degree, the composite system of movements which has become a habit. Its effect on the mind is even worse. It is acquiring a fixed series of motor representations, and "while the hand loses versatility, imagination withers away."† "The spirit of power dies and with it the spirit of discovery and the elevating sense of self respect." We learn, therefore, that "A gradual sharpening of the sense of motion, richness of motor representations, is the general task which an elementary gymnastic of dexterity has to fulfil."† To substitute for such a general preliminary training a manual training, limited to the acquisition of dexterities which will be of direct service to him in his

---

* *How Gertrude Teaches her Children*, vii., 8.
† Wiget, *op. cit.*

future life, is mere "routine education," leading to a
"fractional humanity"—an expression of the *Researches*.

Pestalozzi's views on the teaching of writing before drawing are an interesting illustration of these principles, which
are of course of general application. "Nature herself has
subordinated this art to the art of drawing. Writing is a
special kind of linear drawing, and suffers no arbitrary
deviation from the fixed direction of its form. If the child
has been made an expert in writing before he can draw, his
hand must necessarily have been spoiled, because it has
been set into particular forms before the suppleness
required for skill in drawing has been sufficiently and
certainly established. Further, when drawing precedes
writing, the right formation of the letters becomes im-
measurably easier, and the child is spared the great waste
of time involved in the process of again overcoming his
tendency to crooked and inaccurate forms." *

Drill.

It is characteristic of Niederer that he should have
attempted to fill up the gap noted by Pestalozzi in respect
of an A B C of practical power, and that he in so doing
should have applied a single general principle to the
point of absurdity. In an essay in the *Wochenschrift*,
he approached the problem of a "general elementary
gymnastic" from the point of view of the "elementary
method," a leading feature of which, it will be remembered,
is "unbroken continuity of advance in scarcely perceptible
steps." His physical exercises rival *The Mother's Book* in
the pedantry with which the principle is applied. To find
out the correct order for such a series of movements one
has only to ask : "What movements can I make with every
single member of my body and with every single joint of

* *How Gertrude Teaches her Children*, vii., 68.

the same? In what direction can these movements take place, and in what positions? How can the movements of several members and several joints be combined with one another?" "The range of all possible exercises must be exhausted at each stage." This is a marked change from the running and jumping which are regarded in *How Gertrude Teaches her Children* as the fitting starting points of physical training, and a curious departure from the principle on which Pestalozzi set great store—" that no physical activity is educative which does not spring from an intellectual stimulus."

Although Niederer's elaborate "drill" was published with Pestalozzi's approval, and although, in a letter to Stapfer in 1811, he talks of a "perfected and general training of the joints of the boy's arms and the girl's fingers which shall make the learning of every sort of manual occupation, the easiest of games." As a matter of fact, a very small place is assigned to this sort of thing in the *Report to Parents*, which describes the scheme of physical education practised at Yverdun. "We ascribe the good health of our children partly to their careful nourishment but more particularly to the free active lives they lead." Among the daily exercises which occupy the recreation hours, the first place is given to walking, swimming, sledging, skating, etc. When these are not possible, the boys are led to an open place, where they are divided into groups determined by their physical strength or their inclinations, and there they chose for themselves the exercise or game they prefer. When bad weather makes outdoor freedom impossible, the boys are drilled inside the building, on the lines set forth in the *Wochenschrift*. On free afternoons they take long walks or are put through military exercises.* Formal "elementary"

* Seyffarth, xvii., 50.

drill is at best, therefore, a stop-gap, and is no real substitute for the free movements involved in games. The interest that comes from spontaneous activity is as essential to the physical as to the intellectual side of education.

Practical Training and Actual Life.

We have learned already that physical education, as we understand it, does not include all that Pestalozzi meant by the term. He had in mind the general training in "those dexterities upon whose possession depends both the power to do and the habit of doing everything demanded by a cultivated mind and a noble heart." His aim, in this regard, was to fit the child for the physical conditions of his existence. Clearly the individual requirements in such a matter will vary enormously, and to this fact Pestalozzi was keenly alive. He pours scorn upon a physical education based upon "dancing, fencing, swimming, climbing, vaulting," and the like, the result of which is to make one want to ride when one has no horse, or to dance when one has no shoes, to lead one to spend money and time at the social evenings of the small towns, in which young women waste the hard-earned wages of their fathers, and young men learn to despise the very manual labour which has put it in their power to enjoy all these fine things."* Or, as the same point is put in the Lenzburg Address, "it would be an ill service to humanity if gymnastics brought the children of the farmer and the artisan to such a pass that while they could climb and leap like wild things, they were unwilling to help the mother in the house, and were strangers to the quiet workshop of the father or to the toilsome labour of the plough."†

* Pestalozzi's *Brief Account of his Method*, 1802, Morf, ii., p. 152.

† Lenzburg Address, M. iii., 473.

It was, of course, a general principle of Pestalozzi's that every influence which leads us to apply our powers and activities in a way that turns us from the actual calls of practical life, or puts us out of accord with them, must be regarded as a deviation from the laws of nature, as destructive of the harmony between self and surroundings, and as a hindrance to self-culture.*

Illustrations of these principles occur throughout Pestalozzi's writings, especially in those concerning concrete problems, such as that of the education of the poor. In his letters "On the education of the poor children of the country," whilst he emphasises the importance of games and physical exercises, he lays still greater stress upon work in field and kitchen garden, where interesting instruction in useful knowledge concerning sowing and planting, protecting and grafting, and other garden dexterities is combined with muscular exertion.

In the *Picture of a Poor-house*† which appeared in the *Wochenschrift,* he tells us "the children learn how to run by being set to take care of geese, sheep, and goats, seeking lost ones till they are found, and running quickly on errands. They do not learn to climb on poles set up for the purpose, but on the trees in order to gather the fruit. They work in the most varied positions, they weed, rake, and gather stones; they are given tools early, they carry burdens on their backs and on their heads, they stamp clay on the threshing floor."

These tasks are not set indiscriminately, but in an order determined by their relative complexity. It is an attempt to find a useful and interesting employment for those physical movements which Niederer's drill also provided,

---

* *How Gertrude Teaches her Children*, xii., 11.
† Seyffarth, xiii., 415.

but without exciting the intellectual accompaniment which makes physical exercise educative; it is an attempt to subordinate physical training to the demands of the future, without, however, sacrificing any of that general bodily training, which is as much the absolute right of the poor man's child, as it is of the child of the rich. As partially determining the order of such occupations, Pestalozzi suggests that the exercising of several parts of the body should precede that of single parts; the exercise of the larger limbs should precede that of the smaller, and work which necessitated bodily motion should precede sedentary occupation.

In the case of the more fortunate children who enjoy a home life, the household duties themselves are the best of all instruments for physical education. " The careful and wise use of the means of education afforded by home life is just as important in regard to physical as to moral and intellectual education."* Here, as nowhere else, the practical duties which the wise mother assigns to her children have a meaning and a motive which appeals to both the head and the heart. It is real life, and the nearer the school can approach to it, the more valuable its practical training will be.

Similar considerations led him to draw a sharp distinction between the practical education of the countryman and the townsman. " The countryman who has been sufficiently educated for his position will not need a carpenter to mend every broken board, nor a smith to drive a hook into his wall or to straighten a bent nail." He will understand field work of course, and besides this he will know the use of the hammer, the tongs, and the plane, and be able to do his own repairs. The townsman's

---

* *Swansong*, M. iv., 192.

practical education must rest on a broader foundation. He must not only obtain an insight into the essential features of local industries, but he should receive such a mathematical and aesthetical training as will cultivate in him any latent capacity for invention.

Pestalozzi is always at his best when he is writing in the concrete, when he is discussing a practical issue, and facing actual fact. In such places one feels that it is the real Pestalozzi who is speaking, and that his practical intuitions are often better guides to the truth than his abstract generalisations, coloured as they so frequently are by his mouthpiece Niederer, who had more feeling for philosophical principle than for the concrete child, limited on every side by the facts of life. Pestalozzi in practice never loses sight of the actual boy. The "average child" has no place in his philosophy. "Life educates," and artificial devices which are not based upon that principle are unnatural, and therefore harmful. But "life" is a concrete, limited fact, differing for each individual within other broad differences which mark off the rich from the poor, the artisan from the peasant, the cotton-spinner from the iron-worker, the ship-builder from the mason.

In so far as all are men, having bodily organs whose movements are governed by mechanical laws, a general scheme of physical exercises may be thought out which will ennoble the specialised education for a calling, and assume for it "the pure foundation of humanity," if this general scheme is accompanied by that intellectual preparation typified in the lessons prior to the teaching of drawing. But the "learning time" is short, and much may be done —particularly in country schools—to give an all-round physical training in combination with instruction in the occupations which in all probability will be the children's life-work. Such instruction will have the incalculable advantage of close connection with life. It must not, however, be mechanical. The intellectual preparation is essential, that freedom and inventiveness may be assured. The exercises must be varied, graded, and purposeful, that the "hand may not lose its suppleness," and that interest may be kept up.

Progress in Practical Skill.

Having secured the intellectual foundations and accuracy in the elementary movements, so that their representation for the purposes of development of real power is possible, progress in the acquisition of any dexterity is marked by these stages : (1) correctness of form, (2) power in reproducing it, (3) delicacy in its representation, (4) freedom and independence in its application.[*] When he wrote this Pestalozzi had been convinced by his critics that his A B C of Observation—based on the geometrically divided square —leading as it did to the geometrical apprehension of form, was mistaken.

At Burgdorf, practical work in drawing "began with the horizontal line, and its application to the various objects which lay around. Next came the vertical line, then the right angle, and soon. as the child by easy application of these forms became stronger, the figures were gradually varied." "Every drawing, even the first beginning, was brought to perfection before the children proceeded further, developing in them a consciousness of perfected power, even in the first steps of the art." [†]

At Yverdun, the purely geometrical teaching of drawing was abandoned. The prospectus of 1804, drawn up for the joint Fellenberg-Pestalozzi Institute, does not mention the

---

[*] *Swansong*, M. iv., 239.
[†] *How Gertrude Teaches her Children*, viii., 67, 68.

A B C of Observation and the aim is more to establish a sense of the beautiful than that of developing a sense of mathematical proportions. In 1809, a book of Schmid's was adopted, *The Elements of Drawing in accordance with Pestalozzian Principles*, the chief feature of which was the " unbroken continuity and scarcely perceptible advance " of its graduated exercises—straight lines and curved lines combined in a great variety of ways. The children mastered the elements, copied the combinations, and invented new ones for themselves. Natural objects and drawings of ornament were rigidly excluded. The obvious one-sidedness of such a training should have prevented Pestalozzi from accepting it, but it was another application of a much-loved principle, and Pestalozzi was too little of an artist himself to have a keen sense of artistic error.*

In respect of the remaining school dexterities, we have already noted that the teaching of writing is to follow that of drawing. It will be easy for the child who has gained command of his pencil in the drawing lessons to learn to form the letters. "At four or five he should do this, first with a pencil on a slate, because it is easier to manage than a pen, and because mistakes are easily erased, instead of having to remain before the child, thereby becoming the source of further errors." " When he is familiar with the forms of the letters and their combinations, he is given a pen and a copy-book with graduated exercises." "His first writing with the pen is merely his pencil progress over again, and he should at first make the letters the same size as he drew them on the slate, and only gradually be exercised in copying the ordinary small writing."

He has now passed through stages (1) and (2) of his progress in the art. Learning to write is, however, a kind of learning to talk. When he knows the forms of the

* Rein, Art. *Pestalozzi*.

letters and is skilled in their reproduction, he needs no
more special copies. He has in his head their essence.*
He writes from his own experience and uses his power of
memory and imagination. Delicacy, freedom, independence, are qualities in this art, as in every other, intimately
bound up with intellectual power, a further indication of
the ultimate unity of the whole problem of education.

Another characteristic school dexterity is music, progress
in which follows the same course as in drawing. At its
base are sensory observations involving ideas of " more or
less," that is to say, of comparative length, loudness, pitch,
and tone. " He who has been introduced on ' elementary '
principles into the art of measuring and reckoning has
already got a start towards a clear knowledge of the
intellectual foundations of music." The method was
worked out in detail by W. T. Pfeiffer and H. G. Nägeli,
the former of whom had spent two years with Pestalozzi
at Burgdorf, and published in a book, *The Teaching of
Music on Pestalozzian Principles* (1810). Both men were
doing much for the popularisation of music in Switzerland,
and Pestalozzi invited them to apply his general educational principles to the teaching of music, and help in that
way to introduce it into the life of the people.† This book
was the result. It is divided into two parts ; in the first
there are three steps, in which Pestalozzian principles are
clearly to be observed. (1) Exercises in the observation
of tones in respect of (*a*) their (time) length, (*b*) their
pitch, (*c*) their loudness and softness. (2) The methodical
connection of these three elements—time, melody, and
force. (3) Musical notation.

After this general preliminary training—an "elementary " musical gymnastic—there followed more specialised

---

* *How Gertrude Teaches her Children*, vii.

† *Hunziker*, vol. ii., 186.

courses, as follows : (1) The singing of words. (2) The
relative time and word emphasis. (3) The connection of
music and poetry. (4) The introduction to musical works.
It was only in this last stage that actual songs were sung.
The "elementary" principle has once again been allowed
to overshadow every other.

Manual Training.

The educational value of "manual training" is so frequently urged in the present day that Pestalozzi's views
upon the subject have a particular interest. We have
already seen on what a high educational level he places
manual work, and the point is repeatedly urged throughout
his writings. The school at Bonnal, described in *Leonard
and Gertrude*, Part III., Chapters 66-68, is a school of
industry; in *Christopher and Elizabeth* he writes: "If I
had time and patience and could be a village schoolmaster,
I would take spinning-wheels and weaving-stools into my
school, and the children should learn to speak, to read,
and to reckon, whilst their hands were busily employed."
"Every day the schoolmaster realised more fully how work
cultivates the intelligence, gives force to the feelings of
the heart, and keeps alive the sense of duty." In 1807 he
wrote, "I now regard it as a clear and incontrovertible
principle, that man is much more truly educated through
that which he does than through that which he learns."

We also know how differently he would apply this
principle in respect of the town and country child, and the
question naturally suggests itself as to whether the
principle of work would overcome the principle that is
equally characteristic of Pestalozzi—that school education
should be a chapter of real life, that its arrangements
should always take into consideration the probable
future of the children. With the child of the artisan

and the peasant, work is the starting-point of the whole Pestalozzian system; instruction is fastened upon or developed out of it. In the case of the higher classes, he says, " their children must not and cannot be led through the activity of their hands to the activity of the intellect and the raising of their affections ; on the contrary, they must be stimulated and guided by the activity of their minds to the activity of their hands."*
But the "practical capacity" required by the upper classes is something different from the practical capacity of the artisan. "The power they need depends upon the extent and the solidity of their knowledge, *i.e.* their knowledge of objects and the manner of dealing with them, though for the actual handling they frequently have other people's hands at their call, which they must and ought to make use of."* Doing is not essential, but they should know how to do. "Instead of technique they require technology."†

At the same time, Pestalozzi does not suggest abandoning the "practice of mechanical dexterities" in the case of children of the well-to-do, indeed he laments its neglect as one of the signs of educational degeneracy, but in their case the manual work occupies quite a different place in the system. It is not the centre around which all other teaching is grouped. It is an occasional—though, of course, regular and systematic—putting of the hand to occupations interesting in themselves, or having a close connection with the surroundings of home or school. At Yverdun, for example, the boys learned to dig and to saw, they practised turning and bookbinding, though letters of visitors tell us that this side of the school work was irregular and spasmodic.

In concluding this account of Pestalozzi's theory and

* *Swansong*, M. iv., 280. † Wiget, *op. cit.*

practice in respect of the education of practical power, it may be useful to point again to the intimate interaction of intellectual and physical activity, and to the fundamental unity of the whole problem of education. At the very foundation of practical skill, Pestalozzi's analysis shows us the fundamental character of observation which furnishes materials from which the mind builds up standards wherewith to measure the results produced by the physical activities which it, in due course, initiates and directs to definite ends. Schemes of physical training which do not take into account this intellectual factor fall short of Pestalozzi's idea of the educative; on the other hand, properly treated, the mere "whittling of a stick with a knife" may in the fullest sense answer to that idea. When, however, we regard practical efficiency more closely, it is obvious that the combination of intellectual insight and practical skill is still only a preliminary condition. Without the will to do, skill and insight are lame incompetents. This side of education, the keystone to the arch, is the subject of our next chapter.

CHAPTER VII.

MORAL EDUCATION.

Moral Progress of Mankind.

PESTALOZZI regards moral education as the key to his whole system. "The final aim of education—humanity—is only to be reached by subordinating the demands of our intellectual and practical capacities to the higher demands of morality and religion." He points out that this subordination characterises nature's own proceeding. The child trusts and loves long before he thinks and works. His belief in his mother and his love for her are already lively, strong, and imperishable at a time when he is intellectually and physically powerless. Thus we may say that nature postpones intellectual and practical education in favour of the education of the heart, an order which must never be departed from. Man must be intellectually and practically cultivated, but only by putting these sides of his culture at the service of faith and love can he be ennobled and inwardly satisfied by his education. "That is God's order in respect of head, heart, and hand."

Pestalozzi tells us what he means by morality in the book he wrote at Fichte's suggestion—*Researches into the Course of Nature in the Development of the Human Race.* He there recognises three grades of mankind—the natural man, the social man, and the moral man.* The *natural*

---

* Compare also *How Gertrude Teaches her Children,* vii., 33.

man is, after Rousseau's pattern, a harmless, good-natured being whose wants are in perfect equilibrium with his power. "Man in this condition is a pure child of his instincts which lead him directly and harmlessly to the satisfaction of his sensory desires." "So long as this continues we call him an unspoiled natural man, but so soon as he finds difficulty in satisfying his desires, he loses his harmlessness and his natural good nature ; he is now *a natural man spoiled.* Just as the whole human race began its development as an innocent child of nature, so the development of each child has this state of innocence as its point of departure."

The natural man has neither religion nor morality, and the child at the moment of his birth is precisely in the same position. Like the natural man, " he knows nothing of evil, of pain, of hunger, of care, of mistrust, of feelings of dependence or insecurity." " But so soon as the moment of birth is over the purity of the natural man in the child passes away." His first cry is the sign of unsatisfied desire, of coming struggles and pain which will carry him further and further away from the condition in which God first placed him.

The *natural man spoiled* is in a sad position. Selfishness has taken the place of natural kindliness, and his life is a battle from beginning to end. It is a struggle of all against each, and each against all. He is religious now, but his religion is a superstition. In this condition he remains a long time, escaping from it by means of what political philosophers of the eighteenth century called a *social contract,* under which each individual gives up certain of his natural rights to the whole community in return for the protection which in its turn the community undertakes to give him. This, according to eighteenth century social theory, is the origin of society and of law. *Social man* is, however, not moral. He has no need of morality. His actions are regulated by his contract, that is, by law; and social life is quite possible without any further guiding principle of conduct. But man may easily deceive himself and mistake the actions of organised masses of men for moral action. Such action is, at best, only a modification of natural action due to the obligation entered into under the social contract. Societies may have religion, but it is essentially external—a legal contrivance which has nothing to do with the religion of true morality.

Social man may realise the difference between the innocent independence of his God-given natural condition and his present condition, which is based upon selfishness only limited in its extent by the control of the law. In the midst of it all he feels a need in his innermost self, and the feeling arises that it is within his power to make himself a nobler being than nature and society can possibly make him. Most men are satisfied to live their lives under law. They give what the law demands and take what the law allows. Their citizenship is unquestionable, they live socially well-ordered lives, and socially they are approved. But morality is for Pestalozzi an absolutely individual matter. "No man can feel for me that I am moral." Legality and morality are different in their essence. It is the difference between necessity and freedom. Morality has its seat in the good-will, it consists in the pure will to do right "according to the measure of my knowledge." "Of good works Pestalozzi is sceptical, because he is not sure that they may not be merely legal acts."*

The perfectly *moral man* is the unattainable ideal. Mankind as a whole is as incapable of living upon earth "a life of pure morality as of remaining in the innocence of his original nature." Few men strive after this ideal;

* Wiget, *op. cit.*

social life makes too many claims upon them, and
native selfishness is too strong. But the germ of morality
is in every man, as is shown by that sense of inward dissatisfaction which most men feel at some time or other.
The feeling is an expression of man's true self, the higher
nature which he lost when his desires and his powers
ceased to be in equilibrium, the divine element in him
which is everlastingly opposed to the selfishness of the
spoiled animal nature. Between these two sides of man
there is a lifelong struggle; one or the other must be
in the ascendant, equilibrium is not possible. How are we
to ensure the predominance of the higher nature? This
is the problem of moral and religious education.

Psychological Foundations of Morality: Law of "Natural" Nearness.

As in his treatment of intellectual and physical education, Pestalozzi subjects the "moral powers" of man to a
psychological analysis. He endeavours, that is to say, to
find the elements which lie at the base of moral development, and which are therefore the starting points of moral
training. For these elements he uses the same word,
Anschauung, as he employs for the sensory observations
which are the point of departure for, and the bed rock of,
intellectual education, but in this latter case it is external
observation, the sensory perception of external objects
(*äussere Anschauung*), whereas in the former he speaks of
an inner sense (*innere Anschauung*) by which the feelings
which are native and inseparable from man's soul are
perceived. The stimulus in both cases comes from experience. Upon the one, his knowledge, in so far as it relates
to the external world, rests. Upon the other, that
is upon the feelings of love, gratitude, trust, and

sympathy, which are native and inseparable from his soul, his religion and morality develop.*

The process is the same in principle as the process which governs intellectual education. In both cases the materials provided by experience are "by analogy" made to do duty for new and even for imaginary situations. In both cases the mental impression must precede the word. "Just as in the 'elementary' training of the intellect, the sensory impression of an object must be in the child's mind before the word which denotes the object may be put into his mouth, so must the feelings which lie at the root of moral ideas in the mind of the child be already there, before the words which denote them are known to him."*

As already said, it is experience which provides the stimulus which calls into existence the "inner feelings," but all experiences do not excite them in the same degree, and as in intellectual education, Pestalozzi enunciates a law of physical nearness, which states the ground of variation in the sensory clearness of impressions, so in relation to these "inner feelings" he finds that their intensity varies in accordance with the *law of natural (tierischen) nearness and remoteness*. The fact is reminiscent of the innocent "state of nature," when man's natural inclinations were his sole guide to action, and as a "social being" those objects which lie near to his innocent animal nature are much more effective in rousing moral feelings than those which appeal simply to his sense of duty.

A parent, for example, stands to his child in such a relation. The child is "naturally near" to him, and is in consequence a fertile source of those feelings which are fundamental to morality. In effect, therefore, the law amounts to the statement that the sympathetic feelings are the root of morality. At the same time it must be remembered

* Morf, ii., 159.

that this only relates to psychological foundations. To do good out of sympathy is not in itself moral, but sympathy, operating as defined by the law of natural nearness, provides the bridge which enables the merely social man to pass over into the moral man.*

Of course, when moral objects are "physically" as well as "naturally" near, their effectiveness as agents in the development of sympathetic feelings is greatly enhanced. The "physical" distance of a father separated from his child dulls the action of the law of "natural" nearness. "The mere idea of a father's duty is less favourable to the development of morality in him, than the smiles and tears of his child lying in the cradle before his eyes." Here, then, we have the psychological ground for Pestalozzi's insistence upon family life as the true source of religion and morality. All the objects that surround the child are "physically" as well as "naturally" near to him, and the child's earliest experiences in his relations with his mother are the main sources of "inner feelings," the strength and character of which largely determine his moral and religious future. Pestalozzi never dissociates religion and morality : whilst the one represents man in his attitude towards God, the other in his attitude towards himself and his fellow men, they both have their origin in family life.

In his intercourse with his mother, the germs of love, of trust, and of gratitude are developed in the child. "The development of the human race begins in a strong passionate desire for the satisfaction of physical wants. The mother's breast satisfies the physical cravings, and generates *love*; soon after, *fear* is developed, but the mother's protecting arm drives it away and the child *trusts*. Love and trust united produce the first germ of gratitude." He learns to be *patient* and *obedient*; he discovers that others have claims upon his

---

* *Enquiries*, 148 (Hunziker's Edition, Zürich, 1886).

mother's attention, that she is not there entirely for him, and that he himself is not in the world just for his own sake. Here are the germs of the *social feelings* and of *sympathy.* The first principles of moral self-development are now unfolded, and at the same time there is in them the whole essence of that state of mind which is characteristic of human dependence on God.

The child's dependence upon his mother is the prototype of such a dependence. He is not conscious of the extent to which he trusts in her, and as he develops physically he becomes more and more independent. "He becomes conscious of his own personality and secretly begins to feel that he no longer needs his mother. She reads the growing thought in his eyes, she presses her darling to her heart, and says in a voice he has not heard before, 'Child, there is a God whom you need, who will take you in His arms when I can no longer shelter you.' Then an inexpressible something arises in his heart, a holy feeling, a desire for faith that raises him above himself. He rejoices in the name of God as soon as he hears his mother pronounce it. The feelings of love, gratitude, and trust, that were developed at her bosom, extend to God and embrace Him as father and mother. The practice of obedience has a wider field." The child does right now for God's sake as he formerly did for his mother's sake.* This, however, cannot come about unless the mother herself is actuated by other than purely sensory (natural) motives. She herself must be moral and partake of that divine nature, without which the transition from the social to the moral stage cannot be made. Morality cannot issue from my naturally selfish nature without God's help, and the mother, divinely actuated, is God's first instrument to that end.

As the child grows the physical relations between him

---

* *How Gertrude Teaches her Children,* xiii.

and his mother become less intimate, and with increasing independence he comes more into contact with the outer world. Egoistic feelings and bad examples may now choke the germs of good just stimulated into promising life. " Man's feeling for the right and for duty, for virtue and wisdom, dies out completely when he is surrounded by examples of wickedness, cruelty, forgetfulness of duty, unfaithfulness, selfishness, and tyranny."* The transition period is a critical point in the child's life, and it cannot be left to chance to settle his fate. The whole art of education must be applied "to keep the feelings of love, gratitude, trust, and obedience pure in the child." "Now for the first time Nature cannot be trusted; we must do everything in our power to take the reins out of her *blind* hands and put them into the hands of principles."†

The best of all means is a continuance of well-regulated family life such as that described in the household of Leonard and Gertrude. In this respect the poor have the advantage of the rich, inasmuch as their family life offers so many more opportunities for mutual helpfulness, self-sacrifice, and loving sympathy. No school can take the place of an ideally constituted family, where the intellectual, moral, and physical relations are the most intimate, the most natural and therefore the most educative.

School and Home.

In the exigences of practical life, schools are essential—establishments, that is to say, which exist to carry on the process of education from the point at which the family can no longer undertake it. The transition from the family to the school should not be violent. The school is to aim at continuing the family life, and it *may measure its success*

---

* Seyff., viii., 30-31.　† *How Gertrude Teaches her Children*, xiii.

by its nearness to or remoteness from the family ideal.
This was his guiding principle both at Stanz and Yverdun.
The environment of the home is continuous. The child's
experiences are repeated, not as so many mechanical con-
trivances—such, for example, as those which Rousseau
suggests for the " natural " education of Emile—but as the
outcome of living intercourse.

The relation between parents and children is the model
towards which the teacher should work in dealing with his
boys. Such a relationship makes his example and his
teaching more telling, and only as the school atmosphere
approximates to that of the living room, can corporal
punishment be effective. " Parental punishment rarely
makes a bad impression on the child. Far otherwise is
the case with the punishments of school teachers who do
not live night and day with their children in the purity of
family relationship."* " My first efforts at Stanz were to
make these seventy children feel like brothers and sisters
of a large family, and to make them affectionate and considerate one towards another."

He tried to broaden the children's sympathies and bring
love and kindness into such unceasing contact with their
impressions and their activities that these sentiments
might be engrafted in their hearts, then to make the daily
occurrences of the house serviceable for the awakening of
these feelings, and to utilise for the same purpose, outside
events so far as they touched the household. He taught
them "neither morality nor religion," and gave them few
explanations. The important thing was to establish firmly
that inner sense of right and wrong which rests upon the
feelings of love, confidence, and sympathy; these come
from actions, not from words : they are insensibly acquired,
breathed in as it were from the atmosphere created by the

* *V.* Stanz Letter, App. I.

thousand tender and considerate acts which are hourly observable in the intimacy of family life.

At Yverdun as at Stanz, although the circumstances were poles asunder, Pestalozzi strove to make environment, not formal religious instruction, the chief factor in the moral education of his pupils. In the *Report to Parents* of 1808 he says : " Our educational machinery has only a value in so far as it approaches in character to that of a well ordered house in all its details. Our teachers wake the children ; they are present when they get up and when they dress; they observe their bodily condition and the condition of each garment; they see to their personal cleanliness; they place them in rows twice a day and examine their apparel; they accompany them to morning and evening prayers, eat with them, go with them into the playground, join in their games, take walks with them ; in short they never leave them out of school hours except when they are in bed and asleep. All the unmarried teachers live in the house and sleep in the dormitories." We may not now approve of such unceasing supervision, but we must keep in mind the spirit of it all. It was essential to cultivate personal intercourse between pupils and teachers, and everything which helped in that direction was good in Pestalozzi's eyes.

To lighten the burden upon the younger teachers, they were divided into three sets, so that " house duties " only fell upon them every third day. Over them were the older members of the staff, each of whom had from twelve to sixteen children under his immediate care. He was their school-father and was, as such, held responsible for them. Once a week each of these groups was taken by its guardian to Pestalozzi himself, who in earnest and loving conversation with them endeavoured especially to touch their innermost natures, and to lead them to view their

relations one to another in the spirit of loving consideration.* At morning and evening prayers he talked to the
whole school as a father to his family.

In large establishments, with many teachers there is
great danger of lack of unity of purpose. Boys may be
differently viewed and differently treated by various
masters, each of whom has only partial knowledge. This
stumbling-block must be got out of the way. At Yverdun,
weekly staff meetings were held, in which the teachers
talked over every individual pupil, his progress, his character, his inclinations and weaknesses, and over the measures
that should be taken to suit the particular case. The possibility of one-sided, unconfirmed, and inaccurate opinions
was in that way excluded.†

Pestalozzi regarded the study of the individuality of
children as one of the most important duties of the teacher.
One may lay down general principles, but in the concrete
one has not to deal with a generalised being. The individual is limited and one-sided in his natural inclinations.
He is a problem in himself, and the teacher's first object
should be to find what forces in him are likely to be a help,
and what forces to be a hindrance, to moral development.
This is the meaning of his Yverdun practice, and the whole
tenor of the *Report to Parents* shows the importance he
attached to this principle alike in the intellectual and the
moral sphere.‡

Although there is no talk of an A B C of the moral
feelings (*innere Anschauungen*), yet one finds in the
thirteenth letter of *How Gertrude Teaches her Children*
the idea of a " feeling-series " advancing by " elementary "
steps. He wonders why mankind does not set about the

---

* Compare Gertrude's talks with her children in *Leonard and Gertrude*, M. i., ch. 35.

† Morf, iv., pp. 12-13.   ‡ Cp. chapter v., p. 111.

task of opening out a perfect gradation of means for
developing the intellect and the feelings. On his own lines
he endeavoured to solve the problem for the intellect, but
in the matter of the feelings we only have indirect evidence
of the direction of Pestalozzi's thoughts. In a letter of
Grüner's he says: "I learned from several talks with
Pestalozzi that in his evening and morning conversations
with the small groups of boys, he looked to the following
points: what feelings awake first in the child's heart, and
may therefore be looked on as the simplest and most
natural; which feelings come from the lowest depths and
influence them most strongly; how the feelings which awake
early and those which are easily made permanent, connect
themselves with others which awake later and are more
difficult to fix and make perfect; and how, in accordance
with these observations, moral feelings or experiences
might be reduced to a natural progressive order through
reciprocity in the child's life."*

In any case, however, the environment cannot be ordered
so perfectly as to offer a graded series of stimuli corre-
sponding to a gradation of feelings such as was in Pestalozzi's mind. But in this respect there is no difference
between the merely sensory environment and what may
perhaps be called the "moral" environment. As in the
former case, so in the latter, it rests largely with the
educator to decide to which of the multitude of impressions
the child's attention shall be directed. Clearly there is
room here for gradation, and the teacher's art consists in
determining whether the "moral" circumstances of the
moment are or are not fitted, by the simplicity or the
complexity of the motive underlying them, to be brought
more prominently into the child's consciousness at his
particular stage of development. Mere chance, mere

* Quoted by Wiget, *op. cit.*

"subjective selection," "blind nature's way" cannot be left supreme in moral, any more than in physical or intellectual, education.

Moral Progress: Purity of Feeling and Discipline of Will.

We may now examine in detail how the psychological elements which Pestalozzi held to be the bases of morality are to be worked out. The family and the school constitute the environment which calls the feelings into life, but morality means something more than feelings. In the thirteenth letter of *How Gertrude Teaches her Children*, we are told that through the gradual development of the child's numerous feelings he may ultimately pass to the *recognition and veneration of the moral law.*

As he tells us in the Prospectus, the idea of law comes when the boy is able to distinguish it from the person in whom it is represented, when he accepts it as the guide of his higher nature.* It is a general notion of a highly abstract character, and the school may only be able to carry its pupils one step towards it. In any case, the method is the same as that followed in the development of the general notion on the purely intellectual side. Here, however, it is feelings—(*innere Anschauungen*)—which are preliminary. "The first instruction of the child should appeal to the heart, and not to the head."† "It remains for a long time the business of the heart, it is for a long time the business of the woman before it begins to be the business of the man."‡

In the *Anschauung*-stage, the essential thing is to see that the *right* feeling is roused. Pestalozzi's practice at

* Morf, vol. iii., pp. 185 seq.
† *How Gertrude Teaches her Children*, xiii., 23.
‡ *Ibid.*, xiii., 24.

Stanz is suggestive of the care he took at this point. In conversations with his boys he led them to express their feelings with freedom and confidence. Stated in words, they offered opportunity for kindly criticism, for correction, or for approval. "Activity and purity of feeling must come first in elementary moral education."

But if feelings, however pure and refined they may be, do not find an issue in action they are useless as moral agencies. Morality involves will; and to will involves action with definite purpose and confidence in one's power to carry it through. The sense of power can only be won in action. When Pestalozzi felt sure that the children felt rightly upon the subject of his talk with them, he followed it up by exercises to teach them self-control and to bring the good in them to practical expression.* In a sense, therefore, moral education is a special sort of practical education, and in this way Wiget accounts for the fact that Pestalozzi treats of Intellectual and Practical Education before Moral Education in *How Gertrude Teaches her Children.* "The discipline provided by intellectual and practical training ensures a willing servant in mind and body," ready for the guidance of law when the conception of law is reached. This preparatory discipline of mind and body is, for Pestalozzi, the second step in moral education. It is, of course, to be found in the concrete experiences of school and home.

The immediate aims of such a discipline will be: (1) to increase the power of withstanding the unpleasant, *e.g.*, to accustom a child to submit with good grace to the limitations of actual life, to exercise him in the manful acceptance of deserved punishment, and in cheerful submission to legitimate authority; (2) to increase the energy of the active will. The life of the child in the home and in the

* *V.* Stanz Letter, App. I., p. 189.

school offers two chief means of exercise; these are (a) manual work and physical exercises, (b) instruction.

With regard to (a), what has been said in the previous chapter indicates Pestalozzi's preference. The interest and the immediate usefulness of manual and particularly household work appeal to children. It is an admirable agent for the cultivation of continuous attention. "Work in general is the surest of all exercises for the attention, because it is impossible to do it well without attending continuously to it."* With regard to the more characteristic exercises of school life—those connected with (b)— Pestalozzi has a deep sense of their value as effective instruments for the preliminary discipline of the will.

Again, however, it is a question of stimulus only. "The teacher must transplant himself completely to the child's point of view—step with him from one discovery to another. This is, I admit, much harder than to follow a good handbook, introducing the young people to its contents by instruction, dictation, and demonstration."† But energy of will only grows by its own activity; keen observations, instructive comparisons and abstractions, free thought-activity in fact, leading to independent extension of knowledge, is what is wanted. Only when instruction induces this sort of spirit in the child is it morally effective. The same point is touched on in the seventh letter of *How Gertrude Teaches her Children;* he writes: "That which I gain through the spontaneous exercise of my will in endeavouring to extend my knowledge, my insight, and my practical capacities, has a special value in relation to my moral development.

"But if the energies are directed to any end other than that of doing the work itself in the best possible way, the moral value of the effort is greatly diminished, for it is

* *Schweizerblatt*, M. iii., p. 43.   † Seyff., xvii., 146.

motive which determines the relation of work to moral development." For this reason Pestalozzi will have nothing to do with any external motive such as love of praise or fear of shame. A sense of duty he will admit. The only reward for work done is to come from the ennobling feeling that it has been well done.

In a remarkable interview with Dr. Bell in 1816 at Yverdun, Pestalozzi, speaking of stimulating the child to effort, said that " he never appealed to all-too-easily excited motives like that of love of praise. The children were expected to respond to purer ones, such, for example, as love of duty, of parents, of teachers, and above all love for the subject itself, to which the child must be won by such a treatment of the subject as corresponded to his intellectual standpoint." *

Motives like fear or inordinate ambition may stimulate to exertion, intellectual or physical, but they cannot warm the heart. There is not in them that life which makes the heart of youth burn with the delight of knowledge—with the honest consciousness of talent—with the honourable wish for distinction—with the kindly glow of genuine feeling. Such motives are inadequate in their source, and inefficient in their application, for they are nothing to the heart, and " out of the heart come the issues of life." †

Interest and Wholeheartedness.

" Love for the subject itself," " spontaneous effort to increase knowledge," which the teacher is to inspire, we

---

* Bell was too much in love with his own ideas to see anything in Pestalozzi's, and left Yverdun confidently assuring his companion that in twelve years nobody would hear a word of Pestalozzian method, and by that time his own ideas (*i.e.* his monitorial system) would have spread over the whole earth ! (Morf, vol. iv., p. 330.)

† *Letters to Greaves*, 1827.

are accustomed to call *interest—intellectual interest*, that is to say, as opposed to interest which is only excited by novelty. Pestalozzi attached the greatest importance to it, on grounds closely related to moral development.

" The interest in study is the first thing which a teacher should endeavour to excite and keep alive. There are scarcely any circumstances, in which a want of application in children does not proceed from a want of interest; and there are perhaps none, under which a want of interest does not originate in the mode of treatment adopted by a teacher. I would go as far as to lay it down for a rule, that whenever children are inattentive, and apparently take no interest in a lesson, the teacher should always first look to himself for the reason." Too often " children are punished when the master is to blame." " There is a remarkable reciprocal action between the interest which the teacher takes and that which he communicates to his pupils. If he is not present with his whole mind in the subject; if he does not care whether it is understood or not, whether his manner is liked or not, he will never fail of alienating the affections of his pupils, and of rendering them indifferent to what he says. But real interest taken in the task of instruction—kind words and kinder feelings —the very expression of the features and the glance of the eye—are never lost upon children."

As we have seen, he is concerned to give to the will the highest possible degree of energy, and instruction properly conceived is a powerful instrument in the teacher's hands. It should stimulate cheerful response and lay the foundation of a *habit of wholeheartedness* before which difficulties are bravely met and successfully surmounted.

In providing work for his children, the teacher must make them feel that they need to use their whole powers. " When I recommend a mother to avoid wearying her child by her instructions, I do not wish to encourage the notion that instruction should always take the character of amusement, or even of play. I am convinced that such a notion, where it is entertained and acted upon by a teacher, will ever preclude solidity of knowledge, and from a want of sufficient exertions on the part of the pupils, will lead to that very result which I wish to avoid by my principle of a constant employment of the thinking powers. A child must, very early in life, be taught a lesson which frequently comes too late, and is then a most painful one—that exertion is indispensable for the attainment of knowledge. A child should not be taught to look upon exertion as an avoidable evil."*

A Schoolboy may attain to "Moral Sense," but not to Conception of Moral Law.

So far as mere experience is concerned, nothing more can be done for the child in the direction of moral education. Experience rightly managed is the source of purity of feeling, and experience again affords a field for action in response to feeling. By its means, in the ways indicated, home and school should combine to establish firmly in the child what may be called the elements of a strong moral sense. Unselfish love and sympathy for others, warm-hearted confidence in his fellows, and a humble trust in God, combined with intellectual and physical keenness, should be the aim of his training to this point. "The boy should have an inner feeling for what ought to be, and he should be conscious of serviceable power." When he has attained to the moral frame of mind, when he has been trained in the habit of right action, it remains to produce

* *Letters to Greaves*, p. 130.

in him the idea of moral purpose, through reflection upon the concrete circumstances in the midst of which he lives.

But the difficulty is much greater than in the correspond- ing stage of intellectual training. Feelings are elusive, and words are dangerous, for they come very often when the feeling is not there, and in any case verbal expression weakens them. A treatment which would satisfy a logician is therefore absolutely impossible at the school age. Pestalozzi finds *silence* the essential factor. Writing of his experiences at Burgdorf and Münchenbüchsee in the *Views and Experiences* he says : " What we do in respect of moral education cannot of course be so striking (to the observer) as that which we have accomplished in respect of the intellect. The true moral ' elementary ' education, on account of its nature, leads first to feeling, then to silence, and finally to action. Every distracting and superfluous word tends to falsify the inner feeling, or to weaken its vitalising effect." On the same grounds he objects to the children memorising catechisms of religion. He regarded true religion as a matter of deep feeling, and he believed that in reducing religion to set forms of words, the effect was rather to blunt feeling than to deepen it. " It is enough if, out of the child's home and school life, certain principles, certain views hardly yet formulated, have attained to predominance."

In his actions, however, the child has a more concrete material to work upon. What he has done and is doing every day forms, as it were, a generalised picture of himself in action, that is to say, of the general tendencies of his will. In this general picture he recognises himself, and if he were asked to describe it, it would take the form of a person who in such-and-such circumstances always acts in such-and-such a way, of a person whose conduct has come to be guided by certain rules. In other words, maxims of conduct have been developed. This is what Pestalozzi means, in the twelfth letter of *How Gertrude Teaches her Children*, when he speaks of our activities as being "the sense-foundation of our virtue," and of a general kind of education, suitable to the life-duties of the human race, which "goes from complete efficiency in action to the *recognition of rules*."

From the school point of view this is the end of the matter. School training in morals must not pass beyond "the limitations of actual life, where the transition from feeling to action is easy." Abstract ethical systems must be left to maturer minds.

We may understand now what Pestalozzi means by regarding moral education as the key to his whole system. In the last chapter we saw that intellectual and practical education could not be considered separately. The one involves the other from bottom to top. So, in the course of moral education, we find that he sees in intellectual and practical training the chief means of discipline for the will, and in the acquisition of knowledge the source of its enlightenment. "My morality is nothing else than the way in which I apply my pure will to do right, to the measure of my knowledge and to the concrete circumstances of my life." * Purity of will rests upon purity of feeling, which comes from living in an atmosphere of love and faith, like that tenderly pictured by Pestalozzi in the household of Gertrude, and conspicuously created by him in his own institutions. Effectiveness involves insight and discipline, which come from reflection and action.

* *Enquiries concerning the Course of Nature*, etc. (Hunziker, Zürich, 1886), p. 141.

CHAPTER VIII.

THE SCIENCE OF EDUCATION AND THE TRAINING OF TEACHERS.

What Pestalozzi Means by a Science of Education.

PESTALOZZI's investigations, as described in *How Gertrude Teaches her Children*, are clearly those of a man who was inspired by the true scientific spirit, that is to say, by the spirit of men who place fact above theory, and never allow their anxiety to establish a general principle to affect their judgment in regard to the significance of everything which comes under their observation. The spirit of research could hardly have been better expressed than in the opening paragraph of the sixth letter: " I lived at the highest nerve-tension at every point within the sphere in which I was working. I knew what I was looking for. I took no thought for the morrow, and at each moment I was keenly conscious of just what was essential for the object I was pursuing, but if my imagination carried me to-day a hundred steps beyond the firm ground which I had found, the next day I retraced those hundred steps. This happened thousands of times. Thousands and thousands of times I believed I was approaching my goal, and suddenly found that what I had imagined to be my end was only a new difficulty to be surmounted."

But Pestalozzi saw that science means more than the mere accumulation of facts. He aimed at determining

151

their causal connections, at the formulation of the facts into a logical system resting ultimately upon general principles which would give unity to the whole. He realised that neither an aggregation of facts nor an aggregation of rules constitutes a science. There must be a theory which explains the facts and gives coherence to the rules.

At Stanz, "the whole scheme of a general method of instruction revealed itself to him." At Burgdorf, as he carried his investigations into the teaching of reading, arithmetic, writing and drawing further and further back, he felt that isolated aids to this and that subject of instruction were not enough; they only made him realise that "he did not yet know the true scope and inner depth of his subject." He was seeking a common psychological origin for all those means of instruction, because he was convinced "that only through this could he discover the form in which the education of mankind is determined, through the very laws of Nature herself." The same idea is expressed in the *Report to Parents,* in which he describes himself as trying to drag education as far as possible out of the confusion of its empirical contradictions and raise it to a science resting on indisputable principles.*

He objected strongly to the practice of selecting particular practical points, technical "tips," from his doctrines. "I do not doubt," he says, in a letter to Tobler in 1802, "that the tendency to recognise in my doctrines certain ideas as helpful practical contributions to the art of teaching will be a danger to the doctrines as a whole, but we must strive unconditionally for the recognition of them in their entirety as an indivisible whole. Only in that way can we maintain their spirit and prevent, as it were, my building from being set on fire with torches borrowed from myself." †

* Seyffarth, xvii., 152.   † Morf, ii., 67.

His belief in the ultimate unity of the whole problem is still more directly expressed in the New Year's Address of 1818. There he thanks God that his long experience in educating the children of the people has led him to the conviction that " Education in all its parts must necessarily be raised to the dignity of a science which must find its foundations in the deepest knowledge of human nature." He adds, " I am myself, of course, far from being acquainted with this science. The idea of it is scarcely yet complete in my own mind, yet my mind accepts it as an absolute truth, and the circumstances of the time have made it a necessity for the world." As he says elsewhere, " such a science is the most important of all branches of nature knowledge, the centre of all the investigations of nature which humanity as such is concerned in."*

When Pestalozzi speaks of a " Science of Education," he means a body of principles arrived at by the investigation of human nature viewed as a developing organism, and serving to give authoritative guidance to the practical teacher. The unity of the investigation is determined by its aim, and the possibility of arriving at useful results rests upon the assumption common to all the sciences that the course of Nature is uniform. Over and over again, in *How Gertrude Teaches her Children*, it is assumed that psychical process is as subject to law as physical process. The various expressions, " psychological necessity," " physical necessity," " mechanical law," " physico-mechanical law,' " a mechanism of human nature," " the mechanical form of all instruction," all have reference, as Wiget points out, " to the natural necessity of intellectual happenings," to the law of cause and effect as applicable to mental process.

* *A Word concerning the Present Condition*, etc., 1820.

The Relation of the Teacher to the Science.

But although the teacher cannot override natural laws, he may make them serve his purpose. That is just the difference between his educative activities and those which Nature herself might exert. Nature is "blind," says Pestalozzi, that is to say, the operations of nature are not purposeful ; the teacher, on the other hand, has a definite aim, and deliberately makes use of natural forces in order to attain it. He orders his means to his end, and since the means are in the main the laws that govern mental process, his science is largely built upon psychology. At the same time, Pestalozzi did not distinguish very sharply the physical from the psychical, as the "principles of uninterrupted continuity of progress in scarcely perceptible steps" and the "law of physical nearness" show.

We have discussed already (in Chapter IV.) what Pestalozzi regarded as the final aim of education—the harmonious unfolding of the human powers, the maturity of which he describes in his picture of the man who is all that his neighbours think a man ought to be, a description which, while it lacks philosophical form, really includes all that we are accustomed to include under the word "character." The aim of education is, then, to establish character.

To attain this end the teacher has to make such use of the means provided by Nature as seems to him best, but as the laws governing the development of human nature are fixed, the question may be asked as to whether there can be more than one right way of using them. Pestalozzi says, in *How Gertrude Teaches her Children*, " that he has come to the conclusion that while there are many bad methods, there is only one good one." But he is here really thinking of the principles underlying method, of the psychological foundations which are fixed and unchangeable. He is clearer in the *Swansong*: " We must understand this point carefully—a method of education and instruction which will satisfy completely the principles of elementary education is inconceivable. However clearly these principles are laid down, however perfectly we simplify the means to be employed, every teacher will adapt both principles and means to his purpose differently in accordance with his own individuality."

One man is distinguished by the warmth of his sympathies, another is of the colder intellectual type, and a third tends to view all things from the point of view of their practical application. Inevitably the "frame of his mind" will affect the teacher's procedure.

Equally varying is the individuality of the children, and both in theory and practice Pestalozzi emphasised the importance of doing nothing to crush what is the child's source of strength. The idiosyncrasies of individuals are amongst the greatest blessings of human nature, and should be respected in the highest degree.*

"No institution can, therefore, furnish models of all recognisable methods suitable for all conditions of children, no matter how richly it may be endowed." Even the same teacher may often find it necessary to let principle give way partly to the exigences of circumstance. Time-tables, curricula, unintelligent demands of parents are all facts which have to be taken into account, but so long as he is *on the whole* satisfied that his practice is based on sound scientific principles (*i.e.* is according to the "laws of human nature"), he need not be troubled by external deviations in the form, always provided that these deviations are

---

* See also p. 111 for an account of this principle in application, and compare his doctrines relating to social position and education, p. 78.

consciously made.   He might otherwise lose sight entirely
of his principles.*

Method of Building-up the Science: Experiment.

We may now notice more in detail how Pestalozzi
endeavoured to build up this science.   He was quite
conscious of the incompleteness of his work, and, indeed,
of his incompetence to complete it.   " Whilst I have done
very little in my life to reach ideas that can be defined
with philosophic certainty, yet in my own way I have
found a few means to my end.   These I should never have
found by such philosophical endeavours to reach clear ideas
of my subjects, as I was myself capable of making."
His view that education might and ought to be raised to
the dignity of a science did not come from any à priori
principles as to the nature of mind and the universe.
Although Niederer frequently attributed to his master
current philosophical ideas, Herbart's view is truer, that
it was quite contrary to Pestalozzi's intentions to introduce into his teachings the ideas of critical or idealistic
philosophers. †

* Lenzburg Address, pars. 223-5.

† Yet Pestalozzi is mistaken when he attributes such results as he
had reached entirely to experience.   Although he belongs to no
particular school of philosophy, he assumes all through his investigations that there is a special power of the soul at the basis of every
sort of intellectual activity.   He was trained in the faculty-psycho-
logy of Wolff which held sway until Beneke and Herbart destroyed
it.   Again, in the sixth letter of *How Gertrude Teaches her Children*,
he speaks of the possibility of discovering the *form* in which the cultivation of mankind is determined by the laws of Nature itself.   " It is
evident that this form is found in the general organisation of the mind
itself, by means of which our intelligence binds the impressions
received through the senses into a system."   We have here the pre-
sumption of an *à priori* activity of the mind in accordance with the

Pestalozzi deliberately disavows an *à priori* method; in spite of certain tacit assumptions, one may fairly regard his position as that of the investigator in natural science, who looks upon the facts of experience as the final source of knowledge, and the ultimate test of theoretical validity. "The way of my life is the way of experiments." He took a great risk at Burgdorf in order to have free play for his experiments, and he never let himself be troubled by complaints and criticisms which charged him with sacrificing the welfare of the children to his investigation. His experiments were usually unsystematic, but he never ceased to make them, even after his staff at Yverdun begged him to adhere to arrangements, and not, by "his everlasting experiments, to throw all the classes in confusion, thereby utterly destroying the possibility of connected instruction."*

He was quite frank with the public in the matter. In an open letter relating to the difficulties at München-buchsee he writes, "To run a successful boarding-school was not my reason for beginning my independent work at Burgdorf. I have always wished to be in a position to examine, by means of continuous and sufficient experiences, certain ideas relating to the education of mankind. . . . Although my energies were divided between my new discoveries and the fulfilment of my duties in respect of the children entrusted to me, . . . my method proved its influence upon man's inner nature. At the same time, under the circumstances we could not satisfy completely

nature of which the manifold of experience is synthesised, a doctrine which one identifies with Kant, whose categorical imperative stands side by side with Fichte's transcendental Ego, vaguely and implicitly, in the ethical doctrines which Pestalozzi endeavoured to expound in his *Enquiries*.

* 1813. Morf, iv., 416.

all the general and individual requirements of the children. We did all we could in really essential matters, and here and there were decidedly successful." He goes on to suggest that the division in their work could not, however, continue, and that the study of method would have had to be separated from the conduct of the boarding-school they had founded, that "they were just ready for the change in organisation when the necessity of leaving Burgdorf was forced upon them, and the burden of starting a new institution was placed upon his shoulders." The suggestion that experiment was to be abandoned must have been a momentary concession to criticism at a time of serious anxiety. The teachers' memorial already referred to is proof of his actual practice at a later date.

But although he saw that some positive results had been reached by his own experimental work, he was aware that more remained to be done than one institution under one direction could hope to accomplish. "We require on the one side the freest and widest room for experiments in schools organised for the purpose which would fill up the existing gaps in educational knowledge by the results of their work ; and on the other hand, we require that these results should be tested by daily experience." "For a work of this embracing character one institution could not suffice. We have, for example, the needs of the children of better-class artisans, which, in addition to the more general aspects of the problem of education, call for their particular application to the scientific side of culture ; and equally essential is the working out of a natural education suited to the home life and calling of the unskilled labourers, and finally, there are the claims of the children of the poor and unfortunate who are not in a position to fulfil their duties as parents."*

* *Views and Experiences*, 1805.

Whilst calling for experimental schools, Pestalozzi depre-
cated the hasty adoption of results on a large scale. The
spirit of his whole work might easily be lost in the hands of
a man who, having acquired the mechanism of Pestalozzianism, is set over a large province to reorganise the
schools. In this sense he wrote to Nicolovius, who had
called Zeller, a student of Pestalozzi's method, to preside
over the educational activities of one of the provinces of
Prussia. " The business is not yet ripe enough to be made
applicable to a whole state. . . . I have the greatest respect
for Zeller : he is keen about national education, and he
has a wonderful acquaintance with the mechanism of our
teaching of reading, writing, singing, and to some extent
of language also. . . . But he has not gone beyond a
formalism in which he is fixed and satisfied. . . . The
greater the results he effects in six months, the more
important it is that you should know exactly the point
beyond which he cannot go. . . . Great as he is, he
falls short of the very highest, both in his head and
heart."*

Even Froebel has not suffered more than Pestalozzi in
reputation and in effectiveness from the tendency to mere
imitation.   History is eloquent of the fact that there have
been few good educational ideas which teachers themselves
have not spoiled. Earnest men and women, impatient to
obtain practical skill, take hold of a mechanism which is not
meant to be universal, which is in its very concreteness limited
to the circumstances of a moment, a first approximation,
perhaps, in an endeavour to give a principle practical shape.
They mistake the mechanism for the truth that lies behind
it, become expert in its use and carry it away to be applied

* Results proved how completely Pestalozzi's doubts were justified
in this case. Cp. p. 168.

with absolute faithfulness of detail, but without "the spirit that giveth life."

To some extent Pestalozzi and his assistants were to blame for this in their case, and the less gifted visitors were either disappointed because they could not see through the mechanism of the Pestalozzian formulae, or they saw in them the key to the practical success of the Yverdun Institution and enthusiastically practised "the method" until they could be pronounced expert. Although the master himself saw the danger, as the letter quoted above shows, his example "in never reading a book for forty years" was calculated to make inferior men working with him attach too much importance to their own particular proceedings, and to be, therefore, more concerned to train the visitors in their characteristic dexterities (*e.g.*, in the use of the Alphabets of Observation and of Number Relation) than to inspire them with Pestalozzi's fundamental ideas and fact-regarding temperament.

A conspicuous and not solitary example of failure was doubtless often present to Pestalozzi's mind. Certain Danish students had founded a school in their native country, which in six months accomplished wonderful results in the teaching of the three elementary subjects, but another year saw the end. The teachers were unable to move outside "the elementary books," and the children proved utterly helpless in all matters not covered by them. The public lost interest in the school, and the critics condemned Pestalozzi and his mechanical methods, which were, of course, no substitute for soundness of principle and insight.*

---

* Similar failures in Würtemberg led to a royal edict banishing Pestalozzianism in every shape and form from the schools. (Schmid, vol. iv., p. 600.)

The Aim of the Experimental School.

It was, in Pestalozzi's view, the business of the experimental school to establish principle, to investigate the nature of education in its absolute purity, under circumstances which free the school from the prejudices and private requirements of individuals. By its side should stand the " testing " school (*Probeschule*), and in connection with both should be a Training College in which men might learn, not the mechanism of a method, but the spirit of research. Men who are going to teach cannot be treated like mechanics who are apprenticed to a trade. Each one will have in his professional career a special set of problems to solve, in its details different from that of any other teacher. The best training, therefore, will be given by associating the students with experimental enquiry, with the actual working out of principles and methods, in the course of which they will arrive at the point of view which will enable them to attack successfully the special problems to which in the future each may be assigned. By such a training he may acquire less technique, but he will have gained insight.

Ideas of this kind give the tone to all that Pestalozzi wrote in the last years at Yverdun, and with Pestalozzi, to have an idea meant to strive for its realisation. He felt the need keenly. Hence his appeal for funds in the address of 1818, and his defence of Yverdun in 1820. In the latter document he writes :

" It is obvious that there is probably no calling which requires trained, psychological tact, and the many-sided insight which comes from repeated experiments and varied practice so much as that of the teacher. The material upon which he is engaged and which he must be in a position to handle effectively is the masterpiece of creation— it is Man himself. He must be able to watch over his charge, as a good gardener watches over the most delicate plant from the moment of its first germination to the time of its fruit-bearing maturity. He must know all the child's possibilities exactly, and guide his development effectively in all its directions and in all its intricate relations. There is no profession on earth which pre-supposes a deeper knowledge of human nature and greater skill and adroitness in its management." Man takes the utmost possible pains to understand his dogs and his horses, but there is no institution in which the lofty calling of the schoolmaster can be completely and satis-factorily learned; not merely is there nowhere a professor-ship of the science of education, but there is nowhere an institution exclusively devoted to the training of teachers in the exercise of their profession in the spirit of the best type of family life.

"The experimental school is, for Pestalozzi, the fructifying centre of pedagogical experience "; it is at once the source and the testing-place of theory, the centre from which a higher idea of the aims of education and the function of the teacher may radiate, the means whereby the most fruitful pedagogical ideas may be spread over the widest area.

As Wiget points out, the idea of "experimental schools" was in Pestalozzi's mind some years before he wrote his *Views and Experiences.* Both Fischer and Tobler remarked upon it in the Burgdorf days, and Niederer's defence of Yverdun, after the report of the Commission of Enquiry of 1810 is based upon this idea. Kant, in his *Lectures upon Pedagogy* (published in 1803), has also insisted upon the necessity of institutions of the kind. " Men should first set up experimental schools and then normal schools."

People imagine, he adds, " that experiments in education are unnecessary, and that we can judge from our reason

whether anything is good or not.   This is a great mistake,
and experience teaches us that the results of an experiment
are often entirely different from what we expected.   And
since we must be guided by experiments, no one generation
can set forth a complete scheme of education," applicable,
that is to say, to all future times.   Kant had in his mind
the " model " schools which the Jesuit Felbiger had set up
under Maria Theresa in Austria.   The idea of a fixed
method which still survives in our phrase "Normal
Schools " and " Normal Colleges," and which these
Austrian "normal " schools carried to excess, was as un-
Pestalozzian as it was repugnant to the judgment of Kant.
Basedow's idea, as carried out in Dessau, was better, in
spite of its many mistakes.

In addition to the results derived from his own experiments, he sought to widen the basis of his facts by
inviting old students to send him the results of their own
observations and enquiries.   Thus he writes to Ström in
Copenhagen : " All our teachers meet several times a week
and compare the notes each has made in the course of his
particular work ; the experience of most of them is thereby
ripened and much useful material for our journal* comes
from their discussions.   We are, however, collecting notes
from outside, and we beg that you will lend us a helping
hand, for you live in a circle which might furnish us with
important material for publication.   Send us, therefore,
as much as you can ; in particular historical and psychological notes relating to your work.   It is very important
that we should be able to give the reading public informa-
tion about the progress of our work from all possible
sides."

But important as the accumulation of facts is, a science
must endeavour to formulate its facts into generalisations

* *I.e.* the *Wochenschrift.*

which shall throw light upon their connections, and
contribute to their explanation. Pestalozzi knew the truth
of this. " I naturally at every moment struck upon facts
which seemed to throw light upon the existence of physico-
mechanical laws in accordance with which our minds pick
up and retain outer impressions." His experimental work
gave rise to a " feeling for psychological rules," which he
was anxious to convert into knowledge. But he never
really reached this third step. He collected materials, and
felt the existence of law, but he was not equal to the task
of its formulation. His generalisations, such for example
as his " law of physical nearness," and the abstract reasoning by which he attempted to establish his three elementary
means were not happy. As Niederer put it in his estimate
of Pestalozzi : " His feelings gave rise to an inner conviction
of the existence of law, but he succumbed in the struggle
to derive and express it exactly."

His services in a certain sense may not have been more
than to have confirmed the Philanthropinist idea of a
Science of Education, but his method of confirmation was
important enough to establish his claims as the founder.
His adherence to the facts of experience may not have
been absolute, but in spirit at least that was his method.
He set himself consciously against a speculative method
which lost sight of the concrete child, and emphasised the
necessity of an empirical foundation if there was to be any
prospect of a "Science of Education." He left the problem
unsolved, but at least he pointed to one essential factor in
its solution.

CHAPTER IX

THE INFLUENCE OF PESTALOZZI.

The Humanitarian Motive in Education: Prussian State Action.

A COMPARISON of the organisation, of the aims and spirit, of the methods of instruction in respect of popular education at the beginning of the nineteenth and the beginning of the twentieth century would give a good general indication of the influence which the Pestalozzian spirit has exerted. Although it is true that Pestalozzi was in many respects a child of his age, and that had he lived in the time of Comenius his work would have had even less historical results, we must also give him the credit which is properly due to men who give form and life to the vague aspirations of their age—aspirations which also serve their purpose in affording the environment necessary for the full historical fruitfulness of the master's ideas.

No single feature of popular education has failed to receive stimulus and profit from the work of Pestalozzi. Alike in its general conception and in its detailed practice, there is so much that we now take for granted, that we often seem to be dealing with the obvious when we are reading Pestalozzian principles. We are so accustomed now, even in England, to think of the elementary school as the great nursery of the nation, by means of which the state endeavours to prepare its children for responsible citizenship, that it is difficult to realise how comparatively recently this view has prevailed among the nations of Western Europe. It was precisely this social aspect of education which was Pestalozzi's inspiring motive, and of all purely Pestalozzian doctrines, this is at once the greatest and least vulnerable. The nineteenth century humanitarian motive in education takes its definite beginning from him, not from the anti-social doctrines of Rousseau, nor the abstract theoretical legislation of the French revolutionaries, nor the benevolent intentions of the Philanthropinists.

Heralded by *Leonard and Gertrude*, Pestalozzianism as a social factor of the highest importance at once attracted the attention of thoughtful Governments. Its concreteness was its strength and its charm. It was no dangerous social doctrine which Pestalozzi preached, and Frederick the Great had abandoned the idea that peoples were easy to govern in proportion to their ignorance. The difficulty had been to educate men without at the same time unfitting them for actual life. In *Leonard and Gertrude*, the education is from the beginning intimately connected with the home, directly adapted to the duties the child will probably have to fulfil in the future. At the same time it affords escape for the talented whose capacities would find their best employment in higher social spheres. Upon the Prussian Queen Louisa the book made a profound impression. In her diary she wrote, "I am now reading *Leonard and Gertrude*, by Pestalozzi. How refreshing this story of the Swiss village is! Were I my own master, I would go straightway to Switzerland to shake hands with the noble man, and to thank him with all my heart. How deep is his love for his fellow men. Yes, in the name of Humanity, I thank him."

Not only in Prussia, but in Spain, in Denmark, in

France, in Italy, in Austria, and even in Russia, this book prepared the way for the time when Pestalozzi himself should become a schoolmaster, and after the appearance of *How Gertrude Teaches her Children*, a steady stream of visitors, official and unofficial, poured first into Burgdorf and then into Yverdun from all these countries; it was Prussia, however, that took to the new doctrines most seriously. Even before the great defeat of the German armies at Jena (1806), a Pestalozzian school was opened in Berlin—the Plamannsche Institut—under royal auspices, partly as experiment, but chiefly with the idea of training teachers in the method. In Frankfort in the same year, Grüner, who, as a Philanthropinist, had gone to Burgdorf as a critic of Pestalozzi's claims and had come back an ardent convert, opened the school in which Froebel first found his vocation, and still earlier in Bremen, Herbart had excited a good deal of interest in the work which he himself had seen in Burgdorf. Then came the crushing events of 1806, followed, in the winter of 1807, by Fichte's stirring *Addresses to the German Nation* in which the Prussian people were exhorted to seek national regeneration in the education of their children. Although Fichte criticised sharply certain details in Pestalozzi's theory and practice, taking a general view he urged the Pestalozzian school as the true type.

Prussia was at that time fortunate in its ministers. Von Stein and von Humboldt, who successively guided her educational policy, were full of understanding for the ideas of Nicolovius and Süvern, their chief subordinates, who were keen disciples of Pestalozzi. At their instance a regular succession of teachers were sent to Switzerland not merely to learn the "school machinery," but to catch the spirit of the master. On their return, these men were placed in positions of responsibility over the country, with

the deliberate intention of giving new life to the whole
organisation. Of course their were some failures. Zeller,
for example, was placed over the province of Königsberg,
but through his woodenness and vanity the result was a
fiasco. In Prussia, however, such cases did not stop reform, as they did in Denmark, Würtemberg, Spain, and
elsewhere. Too many officials, teachers, and clergymen
had penetrated beyond the formalism which encrusted the
truths for which Pestalozzi stood, to let an occasional
failure stop the current of reform which was bringing a
spiritual change into the schools.

In 1809, the Prussian state made itself definitely responsible for the primary school system, and laid it down that the
first business of the schools was to train the judgment and to
develop the moral and religious sense, and that teachers were
to be specially trained for their work. Although a great
school system had been organised by Frederick the Great,
it had remained a machine which stood outside the lives of
the people. "Now for the first time the German school was
a fact in Prussia, for the first time it had a genuine
content, and took its inspiration from teachers filled with
genuine pedagogical spirit—the country had become one
great Pestalozzi school."

The example which Prussia had set in the storm and
stress of national feeling, was more or less speedily followed
by the other German states. Still more slowly the Prussian
example spread over Europe. It was not until 1870 that
our own country persuaded itself that primary education
was of sufficient social importance to demand comprehensive
treatment, on the principle of the compulsory attendance
of all children not otherwise adequately provided for.
In the case of Prussia, the emphasis which Pestalozzi
placed upon home training, and the fact that Comenius,
in his admirable scheme for the national organisation

of education, had suggested six to fourteen as the age
limits for the primary school, the lower limit was fixed
at six, and Comenius' figures became the standard for
Germany generally.

Influence upon Educational thinkers: Herbart, Froebel, Niemeyer.

It was not only in respect of the state organisation
of education that Pestalozzi's influence was felt. In
respect also of the theory and practice of education, he is
the founder of a new epoch. The educational literature,
directly or indirectly inspired by his work, is so abundant
that it is only possible in the limits of a short chapter to
indicate its character in very general terms. His own
writings and the books issued under his superintendence
were subject to the keenest criticism, particularly *How
Gertrude Teaches her Children*, and the three elementary
books published in 1803. His most distinguished critic
was Herbart, whose public work for education really began
with expositions of Pestalozzian doctrine.

To estimate exactly Herbart's indebtedness to Pestalozzi
is hardly possible. He was of course a man of different
intellectual calibre, a distinguished philosopher and
mathematician. We know, however, that he was never
ashamed to acknowledge himself a Pestalozzian, even
when in a period of reaction, educational opinion in
Prussia tended to despise the term. He saw, of course,
that Pestalozzi had not a rounded-off theory at his command, but he recognised the value of the work he had done
and was still endeavouring to accomplish.

In his comments upon the Gessner Letters, written in
December 1801, he says that in 1799 he had found Pestalozzi
working at problems which he himself had been engaged
upon as a private tutor. "I had long felt that to give

our children the feeling which comes from clear comprehension was the true object of instruction, and that the only means of attaining this lay in a perfect graduation of the subjects of instruction, a graduation which should satisfy every point of view. This was precisely the problem upon which Pestalozzi was working—the problem of the organisation of the material of instruction, the determination of the order in which subjects should be taught both within themselves and with respect to one another."*

In the Bremen address, "On the point of view from which Pestalozzi's method of instruction should be judged," he says, "Pestalozzi is especially wanting in respect of sound scientific background, and still more in respect of the cool-headedness necessary to the use of a scientific method, or even for the successful mixture and adaptation of learned generalisations out of which orderly prescriptions might have resulted, such as would have been of immediate service to us who would learn from him his art. He cannot, therefore, object to others attempting to set forth some parts of his method in a more orderly fashion, if he has any hope of its becoming widespread."

One may, therefore, conclude that Pestalozzi at least gave Herbart his starting points, that in expounding and criticising Pestalozzi, his own educational ideas were to some extent cleared up. The fact that one of his most important educational publications "Concerning the Aesthetic Revelation of the World, as the chief concern of Education" appeared as a supplementary chapter to the second edition of his book, *Pestalozzi's Idea of an A B C of Sense-Perception examined and scientifically worked out* (1804), sufficiently demonstrates the intimate relation of the one man to the other.

* Herbart, *Sämmtliche Werke*, Bd. i., pp. 141-2.

It was probably Herbart's active propagandism of the Pestalozzian principle that secured his nomination to the chair of philosophy at Königsberg in 1808, in the hope that he would be helpful in correcting the all-too-ready tendency to see nothing in the new ideas but the pedantry which had amused itself in filling a thick book with dull exercises upon the multiplication table. For the rest, Herbart, with a new psychology and a definite ethical system, was able to give to the vague intuitions of Pestalozzi a more definite form, to organise them into a system capable of practical interpretation free from the one-sidedness and mechanism into which Pestalozzi himself was often led through the absence of fixed guiding principles.

The whole literature which has followed upon Herbart's educational writings may thus be said to spring, in the first instance, from Pestalozzi, whose fundamental doctrines so imperfectly expressed but so deeply felt, have been developed into an elaborate system such as Pestalozzi certainly would recognise with difficulty.*

Amongst the many visitors to Yverdun during its most brilliant period, not the least interesting was Froebel, who, first in 1805, on the advice of Grüner of Frankfort, and again in 1808, was studying the practice of his recently adopted profession under Pestalozzi. That he learned very much from Pestalozzi's work is clear. The *Education of Man* is throughout reminiscent of Pestalozzi. As an illustration, one may compare Froebel's early number lessons with the suggestions made by Pestalozzi in the introduction to the A B C of number relations.† Froebel's

---

* *V.* Ziller, *Allgemeine Pädagogik*; De Garmo, *Herbart and the Herbartians*; Rein, *Outlines of Pedagogics.*

† *Education of Man*, International Education Series (Arnold), pp. 81 ff. *V.* also p. 93 of this book.

"Come, let us live with our children,"* precisely reflects what he had seen in practice at Yverdun.

In addition to the philosophic turn that was given to Pestalozzianism by Herbart, the literature of educational theory and practice of a less general and scientific character which had already begun to appear in Germany increased enormously. Men who had seen the work at Burgdorf were keen to describe what they had seen, or to apply what they had learned to the special problems of their own country, and they in turn inspired others to work at some one or other of the many points at issue in relation to natural education.

Even the men who had written educational treatises before Pestalozzi took definitely to the profession, were affected by the new wave of enthusiasm. Niemeyer, for example, whose *Principles of Education and Instruction* (*Grundsätze der Erziehung und des Unterrichts*, 1796) Herbart, in 1802, described as containing the very best that modern pedagogy had said upon the subject,† discussed his own attitude to Pestalozzi's doctrines in a special booklet, *Contributions to the criticism of Pestalozzian Principles and Methods of Instruction.* While the claims of his more ardent followers to the originality of their master are discounted, and the formalism of some of his methods of instruction are sharply criticised, Niemeyer closes with a warm appreciation. "Anything which awakens such a widespread interest as Pestalozzi's educational ideas have done, must necessarily contain, if we can only view it as a whole, much that is both true and useful." "The influence in this case can only be for good, and that in the highest degree, if men will look to the spirit rather than to the letter."

---

* *Education of Man*, p. 89.   † *Werke*, Bd. I., p. 263.

Harnisch, Diesterweg : the Training of Teachers.

We have seen already how the whole educational machinery of the German states were being overhauled; both
public and professional opinion was in course of formation
upon all points of detail and many questions of principle.
The way was therefore open for a more or less ephemeral
literature in relation to the many points at issue.

The question of the training of teachers, of the relation
of the church to the school, of the organisation of continuation schools, of modern types of secondary schools, the
discussion of methods of teaching, the preparation of school
books based on Pestalozzian principles, etc., kept and
still keep the educational press in Germany busy. This
volume of educational literature is a purely nineteenth
century product and is a standing monument to the
influence of Pestalozzi upon educational history.

Even amongst Pestalozzians, it would be impossible to
expect unanimity in a matter which involved so many
traditional points of view. Gradually two wings, so to
speak, formed themselves in the ranks of the reformers.
The left wing led by Harnisch* (1787-1864) emphasised the
need for definite religious instruction in the primary
schools. Harnisch had learned the Pestalozzi method as
a teacher in Plamann's school in Berlin. As rector of
the teachers' seminary at Breslau he did much to work
out the application of the method of sense-perception to
the subjects of the elementary school.† But his church-

* *V. Bibliothek Pädagogischer Classiker* (Langensalza), which includes
the chief educational writings of Niemeyer and Harnisch.

† An interesting letter from Harnisch to Pestalozzi in 1814 is
quoted by Morf, vol. iv., p. 363. It is valuable testimony to the
way in which the latter affected educational opinion in Prussia.
Amongst other things he suggests that an educational newspaper
should be published in Yverdun, that all Germany might be kept in
touch with the parent institution.

manship always affected his view of the function of the school. He emphasised more and more the importance of dogmatic religion, and became the acknowledged leader of an apparently reactionary party, which often appeared to its opponents to be aiming at the restriction of the work of the primary school to the teaching of reading, writing and the catechism.

The leader of the right wing was Diesterweg, without whom Prussian education is hardly to be understood. A stimulating writer, he did much to work out and popularise the methodology of the various school subjects on Pestalozzian lines. In 1827 he founded *Die Rheinischen Blätter*, a journal devoted to the professional interests of teachers, in which for many years he fought for the better education, the better training, and the better remuneration of teachers. In 1832 he became principal of the Berlin Training College, which he soon converted into a pattern professional school. "As the artist is best trained in the studio, so is the teacher best trained in the pattern school. His profession is a practical one. The sharp division of professional knowledge into theory and practice has no significance for him. Pure theory cannot make a teacher. It only leads him astray. The one thing necessary for a teacher's seminary is therefore a well-equipped model school."

In accordance with his ideals, a school was provided in which Diesterweg tried to give practical shape to Pestalozzian doctrine. "The development of the child is to be stimulated according to his own inner needs. Instruction is to begin with observation and to advance step by step to the general notion. The children are to be trained by encouraging the spontaneous exercise of their own activity. The teachers are not to regard themselves as the centre of interest, still less the subject-matter of instruction. The children themselves are to occupy this place; the teacher and the subject-matter form as it were their environment; they are the tools skilfully placed at the service of the children in their instinctive efforts towards development."*

Penetrated with Pestalozzian views as to the great social significance of the school, he fought strenuously against the reactionary tendency which in Prussia reached its climax under Frederick William IV. (1840-1861). Unable to adapt himself to the "policy of regulations" which stifled the freedom of the teachers and destroyed all possibility of educational growth, he gave up the direction of the Berlin seminary only to fight for his cause with still greater zeal in the press and as an elected representative of the people in the goverment of the city of Berlin. The high place which the school in Germany takes, the clear views held by both the governed and the governing classes as to its importance in relation to the future of the father-land, is in no small degree due to the Pestalozzian spirit, as kept alive at a critical time by Diesterweg,* who died three days after Sadowa, July 7, 1866.

In respect of the training of teachers generally, it may be said that the fame of the Pestalozzian institutions at Burgdorf and Yverdun, and the large number of enthusiastic practical teachers and organisers who took their inspiration thence, gave a stamp of reality to the idea which has resulted in the general acceptance of the principle in nearly all civilised countries. Of course the idea was not new. In our own country Mulcaster, in the sixteenth century, had urged its importance, and in various German states teachers' training classes had been actually called into being in the seventeenth and eighteenth centuries, like those

* Schmidt, *Geschichte der Pädagogik*, Bd. iv., pp. 227 ff.

† A selection of Diesterweg's pedagogical writings is published in the *Bibliothek Pädagogischer Classiker*.

of Ratke at Koethen and Francke at Halle. The Philanthropinists also took up the cause, and in Switzerland under their influence, Stapfer made an attempt to create a national system of training colleges. Almost at the same time the training idea was finding favour in England through the successful application of the monitorial system by Lancaster and Bell.

It was Pestalozzi, however, who convinced the Prussian authorities both of its necessity and of its practicability. The reorganisation of schools there included the provision of teachers' seminaries, but the necessity of securing a good general education for the future teachers in the elementary schools, gradually led to the abandonment of the idea that such institutions should be devoted primarily to professional studies. A mixture of the academic and professional elements in which the academic tends more and more to displace the professional, is leading reformers in Prussia back to the Pestalozzian ideal, which demands first a good liberal education free from all professional bias, and lastly, a period of purely professional training. Neither at Yverdun nor at Burgdorf was there any suggestion of such a conflict of aims as a concurrent academic and professional training necessarily entails, to the inevitable cost of both. It scarcely needs to be pointed out how completely the usual English practice has gone in the opposite direction, though recent reforms show signs of a closer approach to the Pestalozzian ideal. Amongst other changes, a new type of training college has been created in which students whose general education has reached a certain minimum standard, will devote their time wholly to the study of the theory and practice of their profession.

School Aims.

In the elementary schools themselves, Pestalozzi's influence has been enormous. The curriculum has been

reformed to answer at least in part to his fundamental
doctrine that the schools should prepare for life; new
methods of teaching have been worked out, based upon
the fact that interested observation is the child's natural
way of collecting material which the mind spontaneously,
though imperfectly, systematises. Lastly, what is commonly called "School Method," that is to say, all that
large body of literature which deals with specific pro-
scriptions for teaching this and that subject of instruction,
is to a large extent the result of Pestalozzi's attempt to
"elementarise" the curriculum at Burgdorf.

The whole spirit of the elementary school has changed.
Discipline is gentler, because the aims are higher, and
because a specially trained staff has replaced the cobbler
schoolmaster of Pestalozzi's own experience. Finally, the
subjects of instruction themselves have been systematised,
graduated, illustrated, and variously prepared for school
purposes by competent authorities who have grasped the true
teacher's point of view. In all these directions there can,
of course, be no finality in practice, but to Pestalozzi we
must give the credit of having put us upon the never-
ending path of progress.

In respect of the curriculum of the schools, we may
note the growing tendency to base it upon the principle of
the spontaneous and harmonious reaction of the child upon
his environment. The difficulty which was felt at Bonnal
—viz., that the school is cut off from the rest of the everyday life of the child—is still a pressing one. The child at
play and the child at his lessons are not, in the full sense,
one and the same person. Professor Dewey's school in
Chicago is, perhaps, the best known attempt to realise
Pestalozzi's ideal, and the questions which guide his
teachers in arranging the school work are precisely the
same in character which Glüphi, with Gertrude's assist-

ance, set himself to solve. "What can be done, and how can it be done, to bring the school into closer relations with the home and neighbourhood life? What can be done in the way of introducing subject-matter in history and science and art that shall have a real significance in the child's own life? How can instruction in reading, writing, and the use of figures be carried on with everyday experience and occupation as their background and in definite relation to other studies," which shall give them a meaning? How shall we adapt ourselves to the individual needs of the children?*

Although few schools have been organised so completely upon this ideal, the dangers involved in completely severing the school from the home life of the children are being recognised, and a system of education which is alleged by its critics to produce "the clerk at the top and the hooligan at the bottom" is being properly subject to scrutiny.

The modern insistence upon manual training in the primary schools is a step towards the Pestalozzian ideal, and Herr Salomon's admirable system of educational handwork in wood (*Slojd*) is a good example of what may be done in this direction. It is essentially a concrete application of Pestalozzianism to the conditions of Swedish life.

Methods of Teaching particular subjects.

As to methods of teaching and the organisation of instruction, one sees on every hand the influence of Pestalozzi's cardinal doctrines. The modern treatment of geography as a school subject takes its standard of excellence from the practice at Burgdorf and Yverdun. In the practical study of the home neighbourhood the child lays the

---

* Dewey, *The School and Society*, pp. 116 ff.

foundations of all future intelligent geographical work. Karl Ritter, an old pupil of Salzmann's in Schnepfenthal, who, with his friend Alexander von Humboldt, shares the honour of having founded the science of geography, spoke in enthusiastic terms of Tobler's geographical lessons. For the first time he saw his own ideas as to the possibilities of the subject carried out in the school.

When he visited Yverdun for the second time, Tobler had gone, but his successor, Henning, was elaborating his ideas, and at Ritter's suggestion the first book upon method in geographical teaching was published. Henning's *Leitfaden beim methodischen Unterricht in der Geographie* is the forerunner of an ever-increasing number of books upon what the Germans call *Heimatskunde*, in the course of which the child not only acquires direct sensory acquaintance with the methods of the geographer, but also through his first-hand observation of natural phenomena—wind, rain, frost, heat, and cold—as well as of the animals and plants of his neighbourhood, is provided with a stock of experiences which constitute a broad foundation for any future specialised work in science. "Look at all things from the point of view of their interaction" is one of Henning's fundamental principles, but his book is chiefly devoted to the geographical side. It was reserved for Harnisch to apply Pestalozzi's idea to natural history for the first time.

Geography is, however, only an example of the way the ideas expressed in *How Gertrude Teaches her Children* have been applied to instruction in special subjects. The teaching of arithmetic has been revolutionised by Pestalozzi's insistence upon a sensory foundation, and although the *Lessons in the Observation of Number Relations*, as worked out by Krusi with thousands of abstract exercises, offends by its mechanical formalism against more fundamental principles, the book was epoch-making in respect of this department of school work, and a new type of arithmetic text-book was not slow to appear, in which the idea of the acquisition of formal dexterity was subordinated to that of training for actual life by means of concrete examples—the truer Pestalozzian view which Krusi, and therefore Pestalozzi himself, lost sight of in their keenness to produce that marvellous dexterity which excited the astonished admiration of visitors to Burgdorf.*

In this way a school of Pestalozzians was formed which insisted on the value of mental arithmetic as " strengthening the thought-powers." Joseph Schmid, von Türk, and Kamerau, all at one time or other members of Pestalozzi's staff, each published books upon the subject which emphasised its formal value, that is to say, the logical training which is given by abstract arithmetical exercises. But even for them, all early work with numbers is concrete, and it has remained so, whatever the views of teachers about the ultimate value of the subject in the higher branches may be.

In regard to drawing, Pestalozzi made the first attempt to bring it within the range of the elementary school. His practical success cannot be questioned, and his psychological analysis of the problem was sound, but his desire to begin at the beginning and to go forward on the principles of the " elementary method " led to the drawing of lines, angles, and geometrical figures, which for long remained the standard procedure in the lower classes of the elementary schools. Pestalozzi had said "Nature gives the child no lines; she only offers objects, and lines must only be given to him that he may see objects correctly "—but the mechanism of the " elementary

* V. p. 205.

method" survived the spirit which gave it birth. The books of Schmid, von Türk, Ramsauer, and Tobler only served still further to stiffen the formal and, to the child, meaningless nature of the drawing lesson. We are now revising our ideas and practice, but the problem of drawing in the elementary school cannot yet be said to be solved.

Pestalozzi's method of teaching children to use their native tongue has become, in its broad outlines, the standard practice of the elementary schools. The child is first taught to speak properly. Through direct observation he learns the right word for the right thing, and when he has got a stock of words which are real to him, he is exercised in their use. All lessons are, at least indirectly, lessons in the mother tongue. Within his range, the child is required to express himself exactly about that which he knows. When he can do this satisfactorily in speech and in writing, the language as such is studied. The grammatical generalisations under these circumstances are as real to him as his own thoughts which insensibly involve them. The passage from the vague to the definite idea in this relatively abstract sphere is now possible. As we have seen, Pestalozzi's own lessons often pursued the formal end to an unjustifiable extreme, but here, as in so many other cases, the formalism of his practice must not blind us to the soundness of the principles which he lays down.

His attempt in this regard, to reduce to order the language teaching of the nursery* in particular, gave rise to much misunderstanding of the true Pestalozzian point of view. Even when abandoning the idea that such instruction should begin with the human body, von Türk, in his *Sensory Perception as the Foundation of Instruction in the*

* *I.e.* in *The Mother's Book,* v. p. 213.

Mother Tongue (1811), applies the "elementary method" to the child's environment with equal thoroughness. He finds, for example, twenty-two different shades of red for the child to attend to and speak in set terms about. The Pestalozzians were first brought into the right path by Denzel, who had worked with the master at Burgdorf, but always took a wide and independent view in matters of practice.

His *Introduction to the Principles of Education and Instruction* (1835) accepts the fact that the impressions with which the child is already equipped when he comes to school must be disorderly, and lays it down that the problem of the school is first of all gradually to reduce these ideas to some sort of form, and to train the child's flighty attention to regard one thing at a time. The whole range of the child's thoughts is in this way disciplined. Then the objects of his immediate environment are brought to his notice in a systematic way; he is taught to notice in them whatever is noteworthy, and he is allowed to speak freely about them. Instruction goes from the indefinite to the definite, from the impression of the object as a whole to the consideration of its parts.*

Pestalozzi's attempt to solve the problem of the teaching of reading was never quite satisfactory to himself, but he never succeeded in improving upon it.†

Lastly, we may note that the systematisation of instruction in music began under Pestalozzi's auspices. The work of Pfeiffer and Nageli aimed at enabling the children in the elementary school to sing from notes, and they applied the elementary method somewhat rigidly to the solution of this problem.‡ Natorp, an enthusiastic

---

* *V.* Scherer, *Pestalozzische Pädagogik,* p. 186.
† It was a purely syllabic method, *v.* p. 195.   ‡ *V.* also p. 127.

colleague of Nicolovius and Süvern, improved thereon in his *Guide to Instruction in Music for Elementary School Teachers* (1813), by introducing songs at a certain stage, since which time the importance of the subject has led to many devices for making it easily applicable to the conditions of the elementary school, not the least important of which is the Tonic-Solfa system, which has, however, so far found little favour in any country but our own.

It is of course in Germany, and particularly in Prussia, that Pestalozzi's influence made itself chiefly felt, partly because he was a German-speaking Swiss, but chiefly on account of the historical situation. In our own country Pestalozzi's ideas were published in the form of a translation of a series of letters on "Early Education" to J. P. Greaves, who has spent some time at Yverdun. The letters were written in 1818-19, and were published in English in 1827, after Pestalozzi's death. We were too much occupied with the struggle between the "national" schools and the Lancasterian schools to be much affected by mere fundamental doctrines. In 1863, however, Herbert Spencer's essays upon education once again brought Pestalozzian doctrine before the English public.

It is not, however, in the wealth of literature that has gathered round Pestalozzi's name in England that we may see his influence. We must look rather to the practice of the schools, and especially to the present tendency to allow the schools greater freedom, in the hope that they may adapt themselves more closely to the home life of the children in the districts which they serve. "Normal schools" such as Felbiger created in Austria—code-bound schools and code-bound teachers, cannot represent the Pestalozzian ideal.

APPENDIX I.

PESTALOZZI'S ACCOUNT OF HIS WORK IN STANZ.

THE following letter of Pestalozzi's appeared in the *Wochenschrift* in 1807. It was partly written during the time he was recuperating at Gurnigel, but, according to Niederer, it was not finished until he chanced to discover the MS. and asked Pestalozzi to agree to its publication in the journal of the Institute. It is important, not only because of the authentic account which it offers of the establishment and conduct of the orphan school, but because, at least in Niederer's eyes, it presents an outline of the moral education which at the time of its publication was aimed at in Yverdun, and might be regarded as the ground-work upon which their whole system of moral education had been built. Niederer published it in the earnest hope " that it might contribute to the right and certain use of such means as are available to the teacher, whether in the home or in the school." "Although it contains no direct practical guidance, yet it is full of principles, examples, and types, the application of which does not appear to be difficult."*

* *V.* Niederer's *Introduction*, M. iii., p. 66,

Difficulties of Situation.

After describing the circumstances which led to the opening of the orphanage, and his preliminary difficulties, Pestalozzi continues : My convictions were at one with my aim. I wished to prove through my experiment, that the advantages which home education has over public education are such that the latter has no value for the human race, except in so far as it makes home education its model. All good education requires that a mother's eye should read daily and hourly, as she lives with her children, every change in the mental life of her child as it is expressed in his eye, in his speech, and upon his brow. The power of the teacher must be that of the father in the purity of its exercise at home.

On these principles I built my procedure. I wished my children to realise at every moment that my heart was theirs, that I was sharing their fortune, and that their joy was my joy. I wished above all to win my children's trust, and to make them feel their dependence upon me.

In this respect, however, my difficulties were really favourable to my object. I had to be all in all to my children. I was from morning to evening practically alone with them. Everything they received, whether for body or mind, came through my hands. Every offer of help, every lesson came from me. My hands were in their hands, and my eyes rested on their eyes. I laughed and cried with them. They were out of the world, they were out of Stanz, they lived entirely with me and I with them. I ate and drank with them. When they were ill I nursed them. I slept in their midst. I was the last to go to bed at night and the first to get up in the morning. At their wish I prayed with them, and even taught them in bed till they fell asleep.

My success was not immediate. The children were not easily convinced of my love. Their old habits were too strongly fixed, and many were disappointed by the necessary rigour of our lives. Sickness and even disease invaded us, and people attributed them to defective arrangements and improper food. However, not one died, and when the spring came everything went well. People were surprised at the change in the physique of the children. They hardly knew them again. Parents were especially difficult, and constantly enticed their children away, but their places were filled again at once. Many of them misunderstood my position altogether : one would imagine me possessed of abundant means ; another would take me for a beggar earning his livelihood by looking after their children. Months went by before a single one thanked me, though the children for the most part learned to know me sooner.

I soon had about eighty children. Most of them had excellent abilities, but they were woefully ignorant. Yet when they realised that learning would be useful they were untiring in their zeal, and in a few weeks children who had never had a book in their hands worked almost unceasingly.

My circumstances made it impossible for me to start with a definite plan either in matters pertaining to the household or in the instruction. The very bases of such an organised plan were wanting and were only to be found in the children themselves, and it was better so. Had I started with the discipline of rules, the severity of external order would not have accomplished my purpose. This would have driven away the children whom I wished to win. I had necessarily first of all to awaken a right feeling within them in order to make them active, attentive, and obedient in matters external. In short, I tried to follow Christ's precept—"Cleanse first that which is within that the outside may be clean also," and, as always has been the case in my experience, the application of this principle brought success.

Family Feeling aimed at.

My point of view led me first of all to make the children feel like so many brothers and sisters, and to regard the house as a real home. On the basis of such a relationship I endeavoured to stimulate moral feeling. I was fairly successful in my object, and it was surprising to see over seventy children of the wildest kind living together in such peace and love, mutual attention and cheeriness, as is rare even in small households.

To bring this about I sought to broaden the children's sympathies, to bring love and kindness into their daily experience and actions, hoping thereby to fix these feelings firmly in their hearts, and finally to make them the habitual motives of their daily conduct. With regard to words, those dangerous signs of good and evil, I attached them to the daily events of the household and the neighbourhood, in such a way as to enable the children to view rightly the circumstances amongst which they lived. But brevity is particularly important, and if I lost a night's sleep in trying to put in two words what others might perhaps have put in twenty, I never regretted it.

I explained very little to my children; I taught them neither morality nor religion; but when they were particularly quiet, I would ask them whether it was not really better and more reasonable to be like that than to be noisy. When they fell on my neck and called me "father," I would say, "Children, would it be right to deceive your father? Is it right to kiss me now and behind my back to do what would vex me?" Or if we talked of the misery of the country, and they were happy at the thought of their own lot, I might remark on the goodness of God in having given men compassionate hearts. At other times I used to ask them whether it was not better that authorities should educate the poor to help themselves than to keep them in workhouses or give them alms, without really helping them out of their misery and putting an end to the burdensome idleness of their lives.

Above all, I held before them the idea of not always remaining in poverty, but rather of appearing amongst other men as intelligent and capable, of being useful citizens and enjoying the respect of their fellows. They began to feel that I would carry them further than other children, to recognise the inner relation of my efforts to their future life, and to picture to themselves a happy future as actually within their reach. Effort was now easier to them. Their wishes and their hopes were in harmony with my aim. Friendliness and virtue flourished in the midst of this harmony, as young plants thrive when the soil suits their nature and the needs of their tenderest shoots. I saw an inner power awake in the children, the universality of which far exceeded my expectations, and the particular expressions of which often both astonished and touched me.

I told them that the neighbouring town of Altdorf had been burnt down, and suggested the probability of there being a hundred homeless children there. How readily they agreed to my proposal that twenty of them should come and live with us! I pointed out that it meant some hardships for them; there would probably be no more money than at present for food and clothes; they would have to work harder and eat less. I made them repeat this to be quite sure they understood, but they persisted in their wish to help.

In the same way I always tried to awaken the feeling of each virtue before talking about it, for it would have been unwise to talk about things of that kind unless they thoroughly understood what they were saying. Such talks were followed up by exercises intended to teach them self-control; that what was good in them might be put to practical use.

Under the circumstances, organised discipline was practically impossible. Such discipline as there was grew up step by step out of our needs. I always insisted upon quietness when I was teaching, and I took pains also in respect of the way the children sat. Both points were helpful. I found in particular that merely to accustom the children to proper bodily attitudes has considerable moral effect.

By following out these principles, the dispositions of my children grew quieter and more readily inclined to good action than anyone acquainted with their general ignorance could have thought possible. But as a matter of fact this ignorance scarcely ever stood in my way, and I found it much easier to treat the absolutely ignorant children than those who had already acquired wrong ideas. The latter were incomparably less accessible to pure feeling than those who were merely ignorant.

Punishment.

When children were persistently obstinate and rude severity was necessary, and I had to use corporal punishment. When conditions are favourable, it is possible to rely altogether on the pedagogical principle which says that we should win the hearts and minds of a crowd of children by words alone; but in a mixture of dissimilar beggar children such as I had to deal with, differing in age and in their deeply-rooted habits, when forced, too, by the needs of the situation to accomplish my aims rapidly, corporal punishment was a necessity, but I did not thereby lose the confidence of my children. It is not the rare and isolated actions which determine children's dispositions and ways of thought, but it is the whole mass of your daily and hourly dealings with them. This fixes their attitude towards you, and in the light of it they form their impressions of solitary actions. That is why the punishment of parents rarely makes a bad impression. Quite different is the position of schoolmasters, who are not always with their children, night and day members of the same household. They have not the advantage of that basis of intimate relationship. They are relatively strangers to their children.

My punishments never produced obstinacy in the children, on the contrary they were quite happy if I gave them my hand and kissed them a moment afterwards. This came from the fact that I was with them all day long, and constantly giving them proofs of my affection. They did not misjudge my actions, because they could not mistake my heart. Others misunderstood me, but I did not mind so long as my children understood.

I always did my utmost to make them understand clearly the motives of my action in all matters likely to excite their attention or their passions. This brings us back to the whole question of the moral means to be employed in a truly domestic education.

Steps in Moral Education.

Moral education, generally speaking, rests upon three points, (1) the attainment of a moral disposition through pure feeling, (2) moral exercises, that is to say, exercises in self-control and effort in matters of right and good action, and (3) the working out of a moral purpose through reflection and the comparison of right and wrong in the actual circumstances of life.

I have already described my procedure in respect of the first two of these steps. My procedure in regard to the production of ideas of right and duty was just as simple and direct. It was still based upon the daily events in their own lives. When, for example, there was a great noise, I appealed to their judgment as to whether it was possible to teach under such circumstances. I shall never forget how free and strong I found their feeling for right and justice, and how this feeling increased and established the kindness of their general attitude.

To this feeling I appealed in every event that concerned the household. A report is current in the village that they have not enough to eat. I ask the children whether they are not better fed than they were at home. I ask them to think carefully and tell me truly whether it would be wise to accustom them to things in the house that it would be impossible for them to get when they left it. Do you lack anything that is really necessary? Would it be right to spend the money I get upon thirty or forty of you instead of seventy or eighty?

Similarly, when I heard from outside complaints of my severity, I asked the children what they thought. My friend, you were there and heard them beg me not to spare them when they did wrong.

I tried to make them set up standards of conduct, to decide what could and what could not be tolerated. I did not talk of freedom or equality to them, but in every possible way I tried to make them feel completely at their ease in my presence, treatment which produced that frank and happy look in their eyes which experience has shown me to be the result of a truly liberal education. I did all in my power to be equal to the trust which these eyes expressed in me; every day I tried to make them stronger in independence, and to keep everything from

troubling those angel eyes in which I found the great joy
of my life. I could not bear wrinkled brows; I myself
often smoothed them; then the children laughed and
avoided frowns in the future even amongst themselves.

Among so many children, I found daily opportunities
of pointing out the difference between the beautiful
and the ugly, between good and evil. Good and evil
are equally contagious, and the greater the numbers, the
greater the possibility alike of evil and of good. I spoke
to them quite frankly about this, and I shall never forget
the impression my words made upon them when, on one
occasion, I had to reprove them for unruly behaviour.
Children, I said, it is the same with us as with any other
household. When there are many children disturbance
causes so much trouble that the weakest of mothers is
compelled to treat her children sensibly and to force them
to submit to order and justice. That is just what I
must do.

In a large household there are many things one cannot
allow which might not be very serious in a small one.
But you must help to maintain the necessary order, or the
house cannot go on and you must go back to your old
miseries. Think what that will mean. Children, in the
world man learns either through necessity or conviction.
If neither can teach him, then he is despicable. Think what
it would mean if you were placed out of the reach of want,
and at the same time you cared nothing more for what is
good and right. At home when you were quite small you
always had somebody to look after you, and, besides, your
poverty at times compelled you to do right, as it often may
even against our will. But to do right on principle is far
better and will carry you much further than what you did
at home under compulsion. If you of your own accord
will strive after the good, in which your highest interest

always lies, you will receive much encouragement from the seventy examples in the midst of which you live.

I often talked to them like this without troubling whether they understood every word, but I made quite sure that the general impression was properly conveyed to them all.

I used also to impress upon them concrete pictures of situations into which faults of various kinds might lead them later. For example, I would ask them whether they did not know people whom everybody disliked on account of their wicked tongues. On the other hand, I would paint delightful pictures of the effects of the good, in particular the difference between a good and a neglected education. Don't you know men who are unfortunate because they were not accustomed as children to think and reflect? Don't you know men who could increase their earnings three or four times if they could only read and write, and can't you imagine what may happen to you if you neglect your present opportunities? Do you know anything more beautiful than to give help and counsel to the poor and suffering? But if you remain ignorant with the best will in the world, this will be beyond your power. Such talks impressed them very deeply, and in general I have found that great ideas are essential even to the first steps in the development of wisdom and decisiveness of character.

Great ideas which cover our whole capacity and circumstances, if they are brought forward in the right spirit, that is to say simply, lovingly, quietly, but forcefully, necessarily lead to a kindly attitude of mind and a ready sense of the true and the good. In this way hundreds of subordinate truths are promptly seized and assimilated, even though they are never expressed in words.

I am above all convinced that wordy teaching, and instruction unsuited to the intellectual condition and external circumstances of the child, often merely confuse his early thoughts. Success depends on whether the teaching appeals to the children themselves as true—not in any vague sense, but from the intuitive recognition of its connection with their own experience. Without a background of this kind, truth is merely an unsuitable toy which bores them.

General Instruction.

As to my course of general instruction, I knew no order, no method, which did not rest upon the children's conviction of my love for them. I did not care to know any other. Thus I subordinated the children's learning to a higher point of view. I wished to stimulate their better sense, and to let our mutual relations have the fullest possible influence upon them.

I had a reading book, but I used it very little. I could not proceed on the same lines as a completely equipped and well organised school; my children were too mixed to make that possible. It was necessary to treat them as a whole. Besides, I attached little importance to the learning of words even when I explained the ideas they stood for.

I started with the idea of connecting their learning with their manual work, of making them run together, but I could not carry out my idea fully because I had neither the staff nor the equipment. Not until a short time before we gave up, was it possible for a few children to begin at the spinning wheel. Further, I was now quite convinced that before there could be any talk of such an intimate union of intellectual training and manual work, there must be a separate general elementary preparation in both directions, and the special nature and requirements of each must first be made clear.

I had also come to the conclusion in respect of manual

work in school, that its value lay in accustoming the children to work, and in making them capable of earning their livings in the future rather than in any immediate profit it might bring. In the same way, I regarded the so-called learning as exercise for the mental powers, and to that end I considered it specially important that attention, observation and memory should be exercised and firmly established before the art of judgment and reasoning was called into play. Only in this way can the judgment be preserved from the superficiality which arises from the facile fluency induced by its premature exercise, a facility which is always more fatal to the progress of humanity than the ignorance of simple people of good sense.

I was, therefore, less anxious to teach my children to read and spell and write than to use these exercises to develop their minds in as all-round and effective a way as possible. I made them spell words by heart before they knew their A B C, and the whole room could spell most difficult words without knowing the form of a single letter. At first I followed this up by letting them read the words they had learned to spell, but later I found it a more useful exercise to arrange the alphabet in combinations of two, three, four, and five letters, introducing all the sounds. Such a series of syllables I intend to have printed as an introductory primer of reading and writing. The consonants were put before and after the vowels, first in two's as *ab, ba, ed, de*; then in three's as *bud, dub, tap, pat, gum, mug.* Afterwards more difficult combinations of sounds as *ig, igm, ep, ept.**

Each set of combinations was learnt perfectly before going on to the next, and at the end whole words were built up out of these elements: *eph, ephra, ephraim, mu,*

* It is to be remembered that Pestalozzi was dealing with German, which is practically phonetically written.

muni, munici, municipal, etc. Each series was learned by
ear, before the children saw it. Then they learned to
write the series, and afterwards they saw it in print.
The writing served of course to double the impression of
the spelling.

As to writing, I spent a long time over three or four
letters which contained the elementary forms of many
others; they also learned to put these together as words
in all possible ways before passing on to new ones. Thus,
when they could write *m* and *a*, they had to write *man*
and continue writing that word until they could do it
perfectly.

I had hastily gone through the sections in the reading
book dealing with history and geography. But without
knowing a single letter they could pronounce accurately
by heart whole rows of names of countries, and they
showed such readiness in attaching what they knew from
experience of the animal and vegetable kingdom to the
technical terms which embodied the general notions covering those experiences, that I was quite convinced that in
my simple way I had succeeded in rapidly drawing out of
them what they had been able to acquire of these subjects
in the course of their experience, and that I was on the
way to completing a definite course with them, which, on
the one hand, would have embraced the whole of that
knowledge which is useful to everybody, and, on the
other hand, would have provided any child possessing
special talent in one or another direction with sufficient
previous knowledge to make further pursuit of the subject on his own account easy. I had done this without
in any way going beyond the limits of their own daily
lives. I consider that holding fast to a principle of this sort
is the best means of discovering talent and helping it
forward effectively.

I always insisted upon the children learning everything perfectly, even that which was quite unimportant, and I never allowed them to forget what they had once learned or to fall below the best work they had once done. I was patient with the slowest, but if a boy did anything worse than he had done it before I was severe.

The number and the inequality of the children really made my course easy. Just as the older children take pleasure in teaching what they know to the younger members of their family and feel proud at taking their mother's place, so my children delighted in teaching what they knew to the others. The feeling of honour awoke, and they learned themselves twice as much through making others repeat after them what they had learned. I soon had helpers among my children, who were really more useful, and useful in a greater variety of ways, under the special circumstances of the institution, than specially appointed teachers would have been. I, myself, was learning with them. Our whole procedure was so artless in its simplicity, that I could not have found a man who would not have thought it unworthy to teach and learn as I was doing.

My aim all through was to push the simplification of all means of instruction to such a point, that any common man might easily be put in a position to teach his children, thereby making it possible to dispense almost entirely with the need of schools for the first elements. Just as the mother is the child's first physical nurse, so should he receive his first intellectual nourishment from her, and I look upon the tendency to send children too early to school and to substitute outside artifice for the home in the early education of children as a very serious evil. My experience quite confirmed these views. I am also more than ever convinced that the sooner we unite firmly and psychologically instruc-

tion with manual work, the sooner a race will arise which
will discover, that what has been hitherto called learning
need not take up one tenth part of the time or the energy
which it has done in the past.   My experience has certainly
established two facts which will contribute to this end—
first that it is possible to teach a large number of children
even of different ages at one and the same time, and
second that this large number may in many cases be
taught they are engaged in manual work . . . .

APPENDIX II.

CONTEMPORARY ACCOUNTS OF THE INSTITUTES AT BURGDORF AND YVERDUN.

THE most objective and perhaps the most instructive account of Pestalozzi at work in Burgdorf is that given by Soyaux, who spent several days at the Institute in August 1802.* It is obviously the record of an impartial observer and clear thinker.

Burgdorf : Pestalozzi's Personality.

He writes : "I admit that at first everything seemed to me so new, and had so little connection with my few pedagogical ideas, that I could not make up my mind about it. Pestalozzi's unceasing experiments give evidence of the extraordinary boldness of his intellect. It was not, however, the elastic, cheerful, easy flight of genius, but rather the straining of undisciplined power. It is a hard and foolish judgment which pronounces him a visionary or praise-seeking reformer. Because Pestalozzi feels more deeply, thinks more boldly, and desires more courageously than the majority of us, he is to belong to the fanatics! Because the old school reforms appear rotten to him, and because, with all the force of his noble dissatisfaction, he breaks through the barriers of custom, in order to fight

* Morf, vol. i., pp. 302 ff.

and obtain for the babes and sucklings a place of exercise where the mind may move with pleasure and freedom, for this reason the ambition of the reformer is said to sway him. Perchance his method deserves little approval; but the *spirit* of his principles, the *tendency* of his method, will certainly have a beneficial effect.

"The machinery of his thoughts is always in constant and strong motion—he lives more within himself than outside—more in his world of ideas than in the world of reality—a spirit of restlessness, an inner impulse drives him sometimes from one room to another, from one companion to another. It seems then as though he desired to chase a flying thought, or to make clear by main force a perplexing doubt. Often the countless visits of strangers make him restless. At other times he passes days together in his room, thinking and writing in total oblivion of himself and his affairs. It is easy to commence a conversation with him; but a stranger is seldom successful in maintaining it and in bringing it to a satisfactory result. Only momentarily does he break the thread of his meditations, pronounce a friendly word; then he retires within himself once more.

" Meanwhile, if one is successful in drawing his attention to real complaints or doubts, he grows lively and communicative—he speaks quickly, decidedly, keenly, with emphasis and confidence—contradiction does not irritate him, but usually only establishes him still more firmly in his own opinion—love and friendship fill his whole heart. It often seems as if he preferred to speak to his friends and pupils through their feelings, rather than in thoughts and words; a hearty slap, a hearty handshake, an affectionate glance, a sympathetic or grateful seizing of the hand, are more natural to him than wordy remarks and superficial communications. Strangers are treated just in the same way as his colleagues, he rejoices in his visitors in proportion as he sees them display an interest in the doings of the school.

"No sacrifice seems to him too great for good and noble aims; altogether forgetful of himself and of his family, he takes many children without fees. He considers it his first duty to be grateful to benefactors, helpers, and friends.

"The decided, independent character of his mind is also visible in the external man. He can lay but little claim to social culture. What he thinks and believes, what he feels and wishes, he gives out unreservedly and in his own fashion. Unacquainted with the forms of European politeness, he depends upon the natural impulses of his mind and heart. He is silent, true, serious, open-hearted, modestly firm, lively without sensory distraction, attentive when sympathetic, unrefined, making no demands on outside help in word or deed. Since he has lived very little amongst people, he does not know how to work directly upon them. He lacks the quiet thoughtfulness, the never-failing sympathy in regard to the small things of life, the certain touch in action, and the social skill of the teacher who knows his way about in the world of children; he knows better how to think than to educate.

Life in the Institute.

"The whole house is in activity by six o'clock in the morning, and in the evening, at the stroke of ten, the young people assemble in a large room—Pestalozzi enters their midst, and holds a fatherly enquiry into their behaviour. Since he likes to be alone at this moment, I did not venture to satisfy my own desire at his expense.

"The little river Emme, near at hand, makes a famous place for bathing, and is diligently made use of by the whole school. In the evenings, in the hours of recreation, the merry throng assembles in the school-yard. The teachers start the singing of a patriotic song, and all who can use their legs march up and down in rank and file to the tune.

"The children enjoy perfect health. Everywhere they breathe pure mountain air, and rejoice in beautiful nature. Nothing pampers their palate, debilitates their body, intoxicates their senses, narrows their heart, or spoils their morals. The daily occupations have so taken possession of their minds, that they think of nothing else but drawing and arithmetic. Even on Sunday they assembled voluntarily in the class-rooms and undertook singly and in groups arithmetical exercises. I often overheard boys repeating energetically to themselves the 'tables of observation.'

"In discipline, the rule is to allow the young people as much freedom as possible, and only to guard against the misuse of it. The compulsion and limitation of *rules* is nowhere felt. Teachers and pupils are as simple and natural in their manner as isolated mountain dwellers. Nothing is known of studied politeness, of fine gestures, of fine-sounding formulae, of conventional custom. The children follow the pure promptings of nature. They do not think about what they are to do. In the full enjoyment of their freedom, they spontaneously recognise certain bounds; obstinacy, ill-natured teasing, quarrelling, etc., are seldom seen. Since the Institute was founded, no punishment has been necessary. There is no trace of 'piousness' or of the repulsive pedantic school-tone. Pestalozzi's principles in regard to moral education are excellent. The germs of good are not unfolded by means of moralising. 'Act before the child and towards him according to the views which you desire him to adopt; put yourself in such a relation to him that he will love you and trust completely in you.'

"Teachers and pupils thus live in pleasure-giving harmony. The former do not dream of expressing their authority by commands, by scoldings, or by encouraging the children to be perpetually dependent on them. They forbid little acts of naughtiness in a gently warning tone; their praise is a glance of approval or a pressure of the hand. The children look up to them with confidence, and never forget the respect which is due from them to a sensible, even-tempered, well-meaning teacher. It is, however, always difficult to steer a middle course. Here, too, this is true. The boys are a little too free. There are scarcely any rules. During instruction they may sit or stand in any order they please; no one pays any attention to that. Naturally youthful spirits have their free play, and the company resembles a crowd that has collected together and struggles for the first place, rather than a body of learners amongst whom lawful order must reign if the aim of the instruction is to be reached.

" On the other hand, the character of the method puts certain bounds to high spirits ; it concentrates the liveliness and claims all the activities of the pupils. Here there is no answering in turn, nor consideration of capacity. It may have its good points that all the boys should speak with one voice and in one tone, but the piercing yells in which they thoroughly rejoiced should not be permitted. At times I did not know how to find refuge from the deafening noise, when it echoed penetratingly from several rooms at once. The ear becomes accustomed to noise, and at last the boys cannot speak at all without shouting.

"The whole household amounts to 102 persons, among whom are 72 pupils, who for the most part come from Switzerland. There are eight Roman Catholics from Appenzel among them. About ten teachers give instruction. To mention several by name : *Krusi* from Appenzel,

Buss from Swabia, *Weiss* from Switzerland, *Neef* from France, *Blendermann* from Bremen, and *Reinhardt*. In addition, there are several strangers here learning the method.

"The institution is young. Pestalozzi's principles are in germ and outline, rather than matured and complete. Therefore one must not yet expect perfect organisation.

"Director and teachers are working with concentrated power at the building up of the whole. One is correcting the 'tables,' the other is following up the tracks of nature in the reading and arithmetic lessons.

"Would that all schools were animated by this beautiful spirit of unity and the ceaseless striving after improvement!

Instruction in the Institute.

"The Institute aims in the first place at elementary instruction, but the period immediately following is not excluded. The steps in the education are connected as *cause* and *effect*, consequently the teaching, the subject-matter, and the method must be thought out in this relation. The pupils are from five to thirteen years of age, usually of the middle classes. The majority are from seven to nine years.

"There is as yet no thought of definite division into classes. There are five or six groups of children, who separate after each lesson, and form again differently, according to their various intellectual needs.

"School books presuppose a certain amount of knowledge and skill, without which they rather confuse than explain; therefore they are banished from the first stages of instruction. Only those who can spell have an A B C book given to them. In every room hang tables (of words, etc.).

"The smallest children learn to count with pebbles,

leaves, etc., and to draw lines on a slate. Others add and subtract the strokes on the first table.* In their first lessons, the teacher, pointing to the table, repeats the process to them until they have understood it. One after the other now comes forward and teaches the rest, just like the teacher; thus the boys learn and teach at the same time. Since the counting proceeds according to definite and necessary rules, the teacher has only to take care that no leaps are made, and that no confusion arises. The more experienced boys are busy with the three other tables* at the same time.

"Here are some problems solved instantly by eight and nine year old scholars; they were set not only by the teacher, but also by strangers.

"Take $\frac{2}{9}$ from $\frac{3}{3}$, how many quarters remain? $\frac{1\frac{1}{3}}{4}$.

"How many thirds are $\frac{2}{11}$? $\frac{\frac{6}{11}}{3}$.

"How many eighths in $\frac{6}{6}$? $\frac{6\frac{2}{3}}{8}$.

"How many fifths are ·7 times the eleventh part of $1\frac{1}{3}$? $\frac{2\frac{1}{3}}{5}$.

"How many times does $\frac{\frac{3}{4}}{9} = 11$ times the twelfth part of $\frac{1}{3}$? $3\frac{2}{3}$ times.

"Of what sum is nine 7 times the eighth part? Of $10\frac{2}{7}$.

"Thirteen times the nineteenth part of 19 times the twenty-fourth part of 24 times the twenty-ninth part of $\frac{3}{4}$? $1\frac{3}{36}$.

"Seven bottles of wine cost 15 fl.: if I break 3 bottles, for how much must I sell each of the others in order to lose nothing? $3\frac{3}{4}$ fl.

* The Table of Unity, etc., v. p. 216.

"If I spend ⅓ and ¼ of my money and have 3 fl. left, how much had I at first? 7⅕ fl.

"Younger and older boys alike reckon with figures, and I noticed that the more practised only wrote down the final results of their mental calculation.

"In another lesson the A B C of observation is given; several boys draw lines, others quadrants, others again divide these into new figures; the most expert draw hands, eyes, heads, etc., on paper. The method of the A B C is as follows—when the teacher says the words, 'I draw from left to right a horizontal line,' the pupils repeat it as they make the stroke. The teacher continues: 'I divide this horizontal line by a dot, into two equal parts,' and so on, until the intended figure is completed. *Then the teacher measures each drawing with a compass.* The boy whose drawing proves most accurate is very proud. Some of them are wonderfully skilful. They draw quadrants in the most exact proportions, as though they had used a compass. One of them copied in freehand a map on a smaller scale, as exactly correct as if he had traced the outline with an instrument. They can describe circles which satisfy every test."

Yverdun: Father Pestalozzi.

One of the most interesting accounts of the work at Yverdun is that given by Vulliemin in his *Souvenirs racontés à ses petits enfants.** He entered the school as a pupil at eight years old. "Imagine, children, a very ugly man whose hair stood on end, whose face was deeply pitted with small-pox and covered with red blotches, with

---

* *V.* Morf, vol. iv., pp. 21-3. Cp. also the various pictures of Pestalozzi at work in De Guimp's *Biography of Pestalozzi.* Translated by Russell (Sonnenschein).

a ragged, untrimmed beard, without a necktie, with trousers half unbuttoned, and hanging in folds over stockings that were down over his clumsy shoes. Add to this an unsteady, jerky walk, eyes which sometimes opened wide and blazed with fire, and sometimes were half closed as if given up to inner observation. Think, too, of features which now expressed deep sadness and now the most benign happiness, and of a voice whose utterance was sometimes slow and sometimes quick, sometimes soft and melodious, and sometimes thunderously loud. This is a picture of him whom we called *Father Pestalozzi.*"

"Him, whom I have just described, we loved; we all loved him, for he, too, loved us all. When it happened that we did not see him for a time, we were quite sad, so heartily did we love him; when he appeared again we could not take our eyes away from him."

"There were from 150 to 200 of us young people of all nations united in the castle. In turn we received instruction and gave ourselves up to happy games. In winter we used the snow to build fortresses, which were attacked by one party and defended by another. There were never any sick ones among us. We all went bareheaded. Once on a winter's day, when the stormwind which blows so icily over Yverdun caused everyone to flee before it, my father, who pitied me, put a hat on my head. Unhappy headgear! My comrades had scarcely spied it when they cried 'A hat! a hat.' One hand drove it far away from my head; a hundred others threw it in the air, in the yard, in the corridors, in the barn, where finally, sent by a last kick, it fell through a hole into the brook which flows by the walls of the castle. I never saw it again; it swam away to tell the sea of my woe."

Lessons: How Geography was learned.

"Our teachers were for the most part still young men. They had grown up under Pestalozzi, and he was like a father to them. Then, too, there were some learned men among them, who had come to help Pestalozzi in his work. The teaching was more for the intellect than the memory; it had as its aim the harmonious development of the capacities which God had given us. 'See that you educate the children,' Pestalozzi would repeat continually to them, 'not train them as one would train a dog, and as children are often trained in our schools.' Our lessons were specially concerned with Number, Form, and Language."

"Speaking was taught by means of observation; we were taught to see things rightly, and in this way we obtained a correct idea of the relations of objects to each other. What we had grasped well, we could express clearly without difficulty."

"For the first elements of geography we were taken into the open air. They began by turning our steps to an out-of-the-way valley near Yverdun, through which the Bûron flows. This valley we had to look at as a whole, and in its different parts, until we had a correct and complete impression of it. Then we were told, each one, to dig out a certain quantity of the clay, which was embedded in layers on one side of the valley, and with this we filled large sheets of paper, brought with us for the purpose."

"When we got back to school, we were placed at large tables which were divided up, and each child had to build with the clay, on the spot assigned to him, a model of the valley where we had just made our observations. Then came fresh excursions with more explorations. Thus we continued, until we had worked through the basin of Yverdun, and had observed it as a whole from the heights of Montela which command it entirely, and had made of it a model in relief. Then, and then only, did we turn to the map, which we had only now gained the power of correctly interpreting."

"Our teachers let us discover our geometry, contenting themselves with merely giving us the goal to be reached, and putting us on the way to it. They proceeded in the same way with arithmetic. We did our calculations mentally, without the aid of paper. There were some among us who gained a surprising facility in these exercises, and since charlatanism creeps in everywhere, we were the only ones who had to appear before the numerous strangers who daily appeared in Yverdun, attracted by the name of Pestalozzi.

"I have said that we saw visitors nearly every day, sometimes famous visitors, who came to pay to Pestalozzi the tribute of their admiration."

"One day he received the visit of a man who gained later a great reputation as a man of science—Karl Ritter—the moderniser of geography. Ritter was even then no ordinary traveller; he was honoured with a great reception. He stayed a week,—a real pedagogic feast—in converse with Pestalozzi and his chief helpers, Niederer, Tobler, Muralt, Nieg, Schmid, and Krusi. Each day they met and discussed education from every point of view. But it was in the confidential conversations with Pestalozzi alone that Ritter felt himself imbued with sympathy and honour for him. He saw that he was in the presence of a nature which soared far above the ordinary—of a great soul of powerful originality, absolutely given up to one idea. In the presence of Pestalozzi's remarkable simplicity, combined with his unbounded confidence in the greatness of the task he had set himself, Ritter felt personally elevated and honoured."

APPENDIX III.

PESTALOZZI'S CHIEF EDUCATIONAL WRITINGS.

The writings distinguished by * are included in Mann's edition of Pestalozzi's selected works (Pestalozzi's *Ausgewählte Werke*, 4 vols.).

1. **Aspirations.** (*Wünsche.*) Published in the *Erinnerer*, the weekly newspaper in which for eighteen months (1765-1767) the young men of Bodmer's circle expressed their political and social aspirations. Pestalozzi's contributions are chiefly short aphorisms in the form of wishes, relating mainly to the moral and educational improvement of the people. Scarcely twenty years old, he begins, "A young man who is of such small account in his fatherland as I am, may not criticise, nor is he in a position to bring about a better state of things. That is quite outside his sphere. Men tell me that every day, but are not wishes still open to me? Surely nobody can take that ill?" He proceeds to wish for a literary and art censorship which would suppress the frivolous romances and poems which were now so numerous as to become a moral danger, and exercise supervision over the pictures which were issued from the press. He wishes that somebody would write a brief manual of popular hygiene, and a short abstract of sound educational principles simply expressed; and that a wealthy philanthropist would scatter them broadcast among the people, and so on.

2. **How Father Pestalozzi educated and observed his three-and-a-half year old son.** (*Wie Vater Pestalozzi anno 1774 sein drey und einhalbjähriges Söhnlein Jacobli unterrichtet.*) Published by Niederer in 1828. Extracts from Pestalozzi's diary to which reference has already been made. Whilst Rousseau's influence is clear, one finds that the story of "Jacobli" being taught neither reading nor writing until he was twelve is a fable. (*V.* De Guimp, *Life of Pestalozzi*, ch. iv.)

3. **Essays on the Education of the Children of the Poor.** (*Aufsätze über Armenerziehung.*) 1775-78.

(i) "An appeal to philanthropists for the support of the Institute at Neuhof." Dated 1775. Appeared in the *Ephemerides*, Vol. I., 1777. (*V.* De Guimp, ch. v.)

(ii) "Three letters to N.E.T. concerning the education of poor country children."

Seventeen letters by von Tscharner had appeared in the *Ephemerides*. They are summarised in Seyffarth's edition of Pestalozzi's works, Vol. III., 237-241. Tscharner is generally supposed to have been the person whom Pestalozzi portrayed as Arner, the good squire of Bonnal in *Leonard and Gertrude*.

Pestalozzi's letters were written directly to Tscharner, who handed them over to Iselin for publication in the *Ephemerides*. (*V.* pp. 24 ff.)

(iii) **Report upon the work of the Neuhof Institute.** Dated 1778, written for the Society of Economics in Berne, and published in extracts in the *Ephemerides*.

It contains a complete list of the thirty-seven children then in the Institute, with a statement of their origin, age, health, character, and previous life. (De Guimp, ch. v.)

4. **Evening Hours of a Hermit.*** (*Abendstunde eines Einsiedlers.*) *Ephemerides*, 1780. (*V.* pp. 27-29.)

5. **Leonard and Gertrude.*** A book for the people.

(*Lienhard und Gertrud. Ein Buch für das Volk.*) Part I., 1781, Part II., 1783, Part III., 1785, Part IV., 1787. (*V.* pp. 29-35.)

6. **Christopher and Elizabeth.** My second book for the people. (*Christoph und Else. Mein zweytes Volks Buch.*) 1782. (*V.* p. 35.)

7. *Ein Schweizer-Blatt.** A weekly paper appearing every Thursday during the year 1782. It was almost entirely written by Pestalozzi; its contents deal solely with social questions.

8. **Researches relating to the Course of Nature in the Development of the Human Race.** (*Nachforschungen über den Gang der Natur in der Entwickelung des Menschengeschlechts.*) 1797.

Most of Pestalozzi's biographers find little that is good to say of this book. Herder reviewed it enthusiastically in the *Erfurter Gelehrte Nachrichten*, 1797, and expressed the hope that it might be reprinted in a more attractive style. The wish remained unfulfilled until Hunziker's edition appeared. (Zürich, 1886.) (*V.* pp. 131-134.)

9. **Pestalozzi and his Institute in Stanz***. (*Pestalozzi und seine Anstalt in Stanz.*) Written in 1799 at Gurnigel. (*V.* p. 184.)

10. At Burgdorf Pestalozzi wrote a number of short accounts of his methods as reports to ministers, societies, and friends. In addition to these he published

Instructions for the Teaching of Spelling and Reading. (*Anweisung zum Buchstabieren und Lesenlehren*). 1801.

This is the book he intended to publish when his work in Stanz was finished. (*V.* p. 195.)

11. **How Gertrude Teaches her Children.*** (*Wie Gertrud ihre Kinder lehrt.*) An attempt to give guidance to mothers in the instruction of their own children. 1801. (*V.* p. 50.)

12. Pestalozzi's Elementary Books. (*Elementar Bücher.*)

(i) **The Mother's Book,** or "A Guide for Mothers in Teaching their children to observe and to talk." (*Buch der Mütter, oder Anleitung für Mütter ihre Kinder bemerken und reden zu lehren.*) 1803.

Only the introduction and the greater part of the seventh exercise were written by Pestalozzi. Everything else was the work of Krusi. The leading idea of the book is founded upon (1) the law of physical distance, and (2) the principle of uninterrupted continuity of progress in scarcely perceptible steps. The mother is teaching her child to see and to name objects—producing thereby *distinct* ideas. The object physically nearest to the child, and therefore the object which will produce the earliest and strongest impression upon his senses, is his own body. The mother is supposed to point out the object to the child and to say the name which he repeats after her. The first exercise begins as follows:

EXERCISE I.

The body.	The back part of the head.	The nose—
The head.		The nose bone.
The face—	The parting of the hair.	The partition between the nostrils.
The right side of the face.	The forehead.	The nostrils—right and left.
The left side of the face.	etc.	etc.
etc.		

The whole of the body is examined on this principle—down to the nail on the middle toe of the left foot.

In the second exercise, the spatial relations of the parts of the body are observed and expressed in sentences as—The head stands on the neck. The face is at the front of the head. The eyes are under the forehead. The nail of the middle finger lies on the upper side of the third bone of the middle finger.

The third exercise draws attention to the relations of whole and part amongst these things—as "the nose is a part of the face," and so on.

The fourth exercise enumerates the parts of the body which occur singly, in pairs, fours, eights, tens, etc.

The fifth exercise deals with the shape and other physical properties of parts of the body, each treated separately; *e.g.*, the lips are soft, mobile, and elastic, inside they are red, smooth and damp.

The sixth exercise classifies the parts of the body according as they are marked by particular qualities; *e.g.*, those which are round, pointed, black, white, red, elastic, etc.

The seventh exercise deals with the most characteristic function of the various parts of the body, the most striking differences in these functions, and the ordinary occasions which call them into use.

Up to this point the exercises have followed the principle of "uninterrupted continuity" in the most literal sense of the word. The seventh exercise, which deals with the parts of the body in action, is by Pestalozzi himself. The subject-matter clearly offers opportunity for more lively treatment, and the author rises to the occasion. To take one example—that of the eye. The section is prefaced by a characteristic appeal to mothers to observe how their infants use their eyes, the delight they take in seeing things, first in the room, then through the window, at the door, and again outside; how they will creep on all fours and chuckle with delight when they reach the object that has caught their attention. This is the prompting of God in the nature of the child, and mothers should follow up the clue this offers to the child's mental needs. Then come twenty pages of suggestive examples. The child is first told what it sees, and, in sentences which are to be repeated by him, he is told what he is doing: he sees, looks at, towards, upon, and through an object, he sees it often or rarely, gladly or unwillingly, clearly or confusedly; "one sees it in a boy when he has been naughty; one sees in the fields whether the farmer is lazy or diligent; everybody looks chiefly at that which is his business—the smith at the iron which is on the anvil, the maid at the milk which is on the fire." "One can see through water, glass, thin horn, amber, crystal, and many other things," etc., etc.

The object of course is that the free exercise of his senses should be combined with progress. The child is to be provided with a wealth of vocabulary and turns of speech, such as formal instruction in language could never give.

In judging of the merits of *The Mother's Book* it is always to be remembered that Pestalozzi regarded it as indicating what might be done, as showing mothers how to give their children language lessons; he did not mean it to be used as a text-book. This point many of his critics overlooked.

(ii) The **A B C of Observation, or Lessons in the Observation of Form.** (*A B C der Anschauung oder Anschauungslehre der Massverhältnisse.*) The book is really the work of Buss. "The child is taught to notice and to name the differences in form and relation between several objects."

Pointing to the horizontal lines the child is told, "These are horizontal lines," and, pointing to the top line, "That is the first top horizontal line." The child repeats this, and learns also to reply in answer to questions, "That is the second, fifth, seventh line," etc. The same occurs with the perpendicular lines. Next they are compared according to their length or shortness and divided into equal parts, to the measure of the first line. For example, the child repeats "The first line is as long as the half of the second line." For correcting the drawings transparent sheets of horn were used, upon which the figures were scratched. After the straight line comes the square, and then the circle. The instruction progresses until the pupil can draw correctly both these figures, without ruler or compass, in the most varied combinations, and until finally he frees himself from the leading-strings of the method by feeling "the necessity for independent progress," and becoming conscious of having in himself the independent power for such progress."—See also Dean Ith's Report (p. 52).

(iii) **Lessons in the Observation of Number Relations.** (*Anschauungslehre der Zahlverhältnisse.*) The book, which was published in two parts, contains two tables (upon which the instruction for the most part hangs). Table I., called the Table of Unity, consists of a large rectangle divided equally into a hundred similar rectangles. Each rectangle in the top row contains a single boldly-printed I, the next row of squares each contain in similar bold type II, the next row III, the next IIII, and so on up to ten. By means of the table the children are enabled to form pictures of numbers up to 100, and of their relations one to another.

In the introduction the book advises mothers to let their children count "peas," "leaves," "pebbles," "sticks," etc., and each time to say "That is (not *one*, but) *one stick*, etc., until through the constant change of *object* the abstract notion of number comes to their consciousness, and they can regard the strokes on the first "table of observation" as pure relations of number, and learn to use them. By means of the first table, the child is to obtain a visual picture of the *unit* as such, and as a *portion* of a sum of units; and again, a picture of a *sum* of units as a unit, and as a portion of another sum, in order thus to be able to compare the unit and each sum of units with another sum of units. This is done in eight exercises. In the first, pointing to the first stroke the teacher says "One," to the second stroke "Twice *one*, etc." and in the same way in the second row, "Two,—twice two, etc.," down to the tenth row. In the second exercise, beginning with the first of the two strokes in the first right angle of the second row, he says, "One is the half of two"; pointing to the second, "Twice one is once two"; pointing to the third stroke in the row, "Three times one is once two and the half of two," etc., up to "Twenty times one is ten times two." The eighth exercise concludes with the words "Ten times ten is ten times the ninth part of nine times ten."

Table II., called the Table of Fractions, consists of two large squares, each divided into a hundred squares. The small squares are to be regarded as units, and the units are variously sub-divided by horizontal and perpendicular lines, furnishing visual illustrations of fractional relations.

13. **Educational Journal** or **Pestalozzi's Views, Experiences, and Means in respect of the promotion of a method of education based upon human nature.*** 1807. Printed in Mann's edition as *Ansichten und Erfahrungen die Idee der Elementarbildung betreffend.* The only number of a second journal projected by the Institute. Written in the interval between Münchenbüchsee and Yverdun. Like *How Gertrude Teaches her Children*, it takes the form of a series of letters (8). Six of these—Nos. 3 to 8—are part of a larger plan to publish a revised edition of the Gessner letters, which should take account of the advances he had made since that book appeared. The MS. of the whole, if it ever existed, is now lost. It contains an interesting review of his life-work up to the time of writing, and a forecast of what he hopes may come in the

future.   Many of his principles are set forth with greater
clearness than in any other of his writings; *e.g.*, his views
on moral education and on the need for experimental
schools (*v.* p. 158).

14. *Wochenschrift für Menschenbildung,** 1806-1810 (*v.* p. 60).

The Stanz Letter, the *Report to Parents,* and the Lenzburg Address are the most important writings that
appeared in the *Wochenschrift*.   The **Lenzburg Address*** was
written as a reply to many criticisms which had been
directed against the Institute at Yverdun.   It opens with
an appeal to the critics to come and see.   He calls his
method " the organic-genetic elementary method which
aims at seeking out and establishing the unchangeable
starting points and the unchangeable lines of progress in
all instruction and education."   It is an unconditional
principle of the method that it cannot put into the child
what is not already there in germ.   The child is made in
God's image.   He is not a *tabula rasa* on which one may
write from without, nor is he an empty barrel which has
to be filled with strange matter, but a real, living, self-
active power which from the first moment of its existence
is busied with its own development, using the materials
presented to it by circumstance to that end.

In this regard, this method is *positive*.   It is not occupied
in preventing the development of the bad, but in actively
stimulating the good, thereby indirectly keeping down
weakness and error.   The teacher inspired by the method
is too conscious of his own weaknesses to wish to interfere
forcefully in the boy's development.   His particular part
is to bring to birth the child's human and intellectual
independence, in other words his individuality.   The
individuality of the child must always be the starting point
of his procedure.

The method is *positive* also in respect of instruction.   It presupposes that all branches of human knowledge have starting points, and it endeavours to seek them out. From this point of view the method is *general*, not however in the sense that it treats all men alike irrespective of powers, character, and position.

The mother is the natural type of an educator who follows this method, and the art of elementary education consists in an uninterrupted continuation of the mother's methods in all the directions education takes.

As Christianity belongs to us all, rich or poor, so is elementary intellectual education applicable to all men. Even the poorest of men may by its means be raised to the highest development of the powers which God has given him.

The method declines to use such feelings as love of honour and emulation. The child brought up on its principles compares himself with nobody but himself. Those who have seen his boys in the moment when they have finished a particular task, will quite realise that no such stimulus to effort is necessary. The same spirit rules in play-ground and school alike.

The method rests absolutely upon love. It recognises no forms of intellectual, physical, or moral education, which do not find in love and faith a common point of agreement.

After pointing out the difficulties to be overcome in practice, Pestalozzi once again outlines the development of the child as Nature and a good mother would determine it, though he admits finally that such mothers are rare.

15. "Report to the Parents and the Public concerning the present condition and arrangements of the Pestalozzian Institute at Yverdun." (*Bericht an die Eltern und das Publikum über des gegenwärtigen Zustand . . . der Anstalt.*) 1808 in the *Wochenschrift.* (*V.* pp. 61, 111, 120.)

16. **Pestalozzi's Addresses.*** It was Pestalozzi's custom to

address the whole school in a more formal way on special occasions. Some of these addresses have been lost, but we have still over twenty. The chief are the new year and birthday addresses of 1808, 1809, 1810, 1811, 1812, 1818.

It is impossible to summarise these eloquent addresses which mirror so faithfully Pestalozzi's moods at the time they were uttered, and show clearly his humble trust in God and his unconquerable belief in his ideals. The address of 1818 is specially interesting, as it contains Pestalozzi's appeal for funds to establish a great educational institute. (*V.* p. 65.) A not dissimilar appeal was printed in English as "The Address of Pestalozzi to the British public soliciting them to aid by subscriptions his plan of preparing schoolmasters and mistresses for the people, that mankind may in time receive the first principles of intellectual instruction from their Mothers" (Sept. 1818).

17. **Swansong.** (*Schwanengesang.*) This work, which was not published until 1826, was written in the period 1811-13. It is divided into two parts—the first part is a re-statement of Pestalozzi's doctrines intended originally for separate publication under the title "Education according to Nature" (*Uber die Naturgemässheit der Erziehung*). It occupies about two-thirds of the *Swansong.* The second part he intended to publish as a message from "The sick Pestalozzi to the healthy public." It is in the nature of an apology for the failure of his efforts to realise his own ideals.

The work opens with a discussion of the meaning of elementary education. He defines it as the result of the efforts of humanity to offer such guidance to the course of nature in the unfolding of the capacities and powers as would confer upon the individual the enlightened love, the cultivated intelligence, and the practical good sense of the race.

He then asks and discusses the answers to the three questions :

(1) How do the bases of our moral life—Faith and Love—actually and naturally reveal themselves in humanity?

(2) How do the bases of our intellectual life, of our thought powers, naturally unfold?

(3) How do the bases of our practical capacity reveal themselves in nature—the power, that is to say, by means of which we give expression to the results of our intellectual activity, and successful effect to the impulses of our hearts, and upon the cultivation of which our domestic and civic efficiency depends.

A perfect scheme of elementary education exists nowhere, and he sums up the results of his own researches into the practical means which bear upon it, in the principle: "Life Educates." He examines this principle and sets forth its truth in respect of intellectual, moral, and practical education.

The educational value of subjects of instruction—history and geography being taken as types, the meaning of human nature which is not a mere conglomeration of powers, the education suited to particular social rank, and the necessity of organising education on a religious basis, are then each in turn discussed.

In the last part of the *Swansong* he endeavours to sum up the results of his work. He recognises its incompleteness, but he feels still that some good has come from his efforts at Burgdorf and Yverdun. He closes his review with the words "Examine everything, hold to that which is good, and if you conceive anything better, add it to that which I, in truth and love, have endeavoured to give you in these pages, and, at any rate, do not cast aside the whole of my life's effort as a thing of the past, deserving no further attention."

18. **A Word concerning the present Condition of my Pedagogical Efforts and the new Organisation of my Institute.** (*Ein Wort über den gegenwärtigen Zustand meiner pädagogischer Bestrebungen. . . .*) It is in part an explanation of the changes brought about by the re-union of the Institute at Clendy with that of Yverdun. (*V.* also p. 66.)

19. **Life's Destiny.** (*Lebensschicksal.*) 1826. Written and published after Yverdun was closed. Pestalozzi's last work, in which he enters into the painful details of the quarrel between Schmid and himself on the one side, and Niederer and Krusi on the other. An unhappy publication which all Pestalozzi's friends regretted.

20. **Letters on Early Education.** Addressed to J. P. Greaves, Esq., in 1818, and published in translation in 1827. Thirty-four letters referring chiefly to mothers' education of their children. Now out of print. (See also pp. 146-8.)